Mastering Spring Boot

From Basics to Advanced Concepts – A Practical Guide for Java Developers

Aneesh Kumar

ABOUT THE AUTHOR

Aneesh Kumar

Aneesh Kumar, hailing from the picturesque state of Kerala, India, is a seasoned software developer with over 15 years of experience. His expertise spans across Java, Spring Boot, DevOps, databases, and software design, making him a trusted authority in modern software development practices. Aneesh's dedication to sharing knowledge has inspired countless developers through his in-depth tutorials and articles. "Mastering Spring Boot" is a testament to his passion for teaching and his commitment to helping others excel in the world of Spring Boot development.

CONTENTS

INTRODUCTION

Welcome to the **Mastering Spring Boot : From Basics to Advanced Concepts - A Practical Guide for Java Developers**. This eBook is designed to be your ultimate resource for mastering Spring Boot, the powerful and highly popular framework that has revolutionized the way developers build Java-based applications. Whether you are just starting your journey into the Spring ecosystem or are an experienced developer aiming to refine your skills, this guide is structured to provide value at every step.

Spring Boot simplifies application development by eliminating boilerplate code and providing a robust ecosystem for building production-ready applications. In this eBook, we begin with the basics, covering foundational concepts like dependency injection, configuration, and setting up a project. As you progress, we delve into more advanced topics like building REST APIs, integrating databases with JPA and Hibernate, implementing security, and handling messaging systems like Kafka and RabbitMQ.

This masterclass takes a hands-on approach, following a consistent Student Management API example throughout the series to demonstrate concepts in action. You'll see step-by-step code examples with detailed explanations, ensuring that you not only learn the "how" but also the "why" behind every implementation. By the end of this eBook, you'll have a solid understanding of Spring Boot and its capabilities to build scalable, maintainable, and high-performance applications for modern use cases.

Whether your goal is to build microservices, integrate third-party APIs, or deploy your applications to the cloud, this guide equips you with the skills and knowledge to excel. Get ready to dive deep into the world of Spring Boot and transform your approach to Java development. Let's get started!

CHAPTER I

INTRODUCTION TO SPRING BOOT

What is Spring Boot?

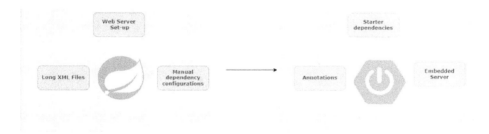

Traditional Spring Frameworks   **Spring Boot**

Spring Boot is a framework that simplifies Spring-based Java. While traditional Spring applications require extensive configuration, Spring Boot offers a more convenient and minimalistic approach.

With Spring Boot, you don't need to worry about these efforts:

- Manually setting up dependency configurations
- Writing long XML files
- Tediously setting up web servers

Spring Boot comes with auto-configuration, which automatically sets up the required components for your application according to the dependencies you add in your build file.

Spring Boot also provides annotations which completely removes the need of writing XMLs for bean creations.

Spring Boot also provides an embedded server (such as Tomcat, Jetty, or Undertow), meaning you can run your application as a standalone executable JAR file.

Why Spring Boot?

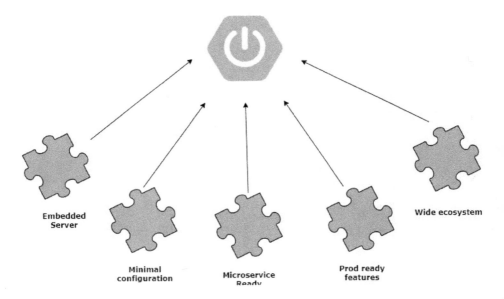

Here are some compelling reasons why Spring Boot has become the go-to framework for many Java developers:

- **Minimal Configuration**: Spring Boot's auto-configuration eliminates the need to manually configure things like database connections, dependency injections, or web server settings. This makes development faster and easier. It can be done just by adding a special dependency category called "starter dependency". This starter dependency will automatically download the required dependencies and add them to your Spring Boot project. For example, starter-web dependency will make your application ready for REST web services.
- **Microservice Ready:** Spring Boot is an excellent option for Microservice applications as it provides all required configurations. Also as it comes with an embedded server, it is ideal for creating and running microservices. Docker-related capabilities also come with Spring Boot so the applications can be also made Docker-ready easily. With these capabilities, Spring Boot provides you with all the tools to build independent, deployable services.

- **Embedded Server:** With Spring Boot, you don't need to worry about the web server for your application deployment. You can run your application just by packaging the project code as a jar and executing the jar with a simple command line program.
- **Production-Ready Features:** Spring Boot also comes with built-in monitoring, health checks, and performance metrics via Spring Boot Actuator, which is crucial for managing production systems. You just need to add the actuator dependency in your build file.
- **Wide Ecosystem:** The Spring ecosystem is vast, and Spring Boot allows easy integration with other Spring projects such as Spring Data, Spring Security, and Spring Cloud. Again these integrations can be done by adding relevant starter dependencies in the build file.

Key Features of Spring Boot

- **Auto-Configuration:** Spring Boot automatically configures your application based on dependencies mentioned in build files.
- **Spring Initializr:** A web-based tool (and also accessible via IDEs) that helps you create Spring Boot projects quickly by selecting the required dependencies using the user interface. After selecting the required dependencies, you can just download the project as a zip file.
- **Spring Boot CLI:** A command-line interface for quickly developing Spring applications using Groovy.
- **Embedded Servers:** As already mentioned, Spring Boot includes an embedded server, so you don't have to install a separate web server.
- **Spring Boot Actuator:** Provides essential production-ready features like monitoring, health checks, and metrics.

How Spring Boot Simplifies Development

Let's take a quick comparison. In a traditional Spring application, setting up a web application required:
- Multiple configuration files (often XML or Java-based configuration)
- Setting up a web.xml file to configure servlets
- Manually deploying your WAR files to a server like Tomcat

With Spring Boot, however, much of this setup is done automatically. Instead of configuring a web server, you simply include the spring-boot-starter-web dependency, and Spring Boot will:

- Start up an embedded Tomcat server for you
- Handle request routing via its built-in dispatcher servlet
- Set up any necessary beans or services, based on the dependencies you've included

You can go from zero to running an application in minutes with just a few lines of code.

Getting Started with Spring Boot

Spring Boot makes getting started incredibly easy. One of the best ways to create a new project is through the Spring Initializr, which you can find at start.spring.io. Here's how you can create your first Spring Boot project in just a few simple steps:

- **Go to Spring Initializr**: Visit start.spring.io and select your project settings like:
  - Project Type (Maven or Gradle)
  - Language (Java, Kotlin, or Groovy)
  - Spring Boot version
  - Dependencies (such as Spring Web, Spring Data, or Thymeleaf)

- **Download the Project**: Once you've configured your project, you can download the generated zip file.
- **Import into Your IDE**: Open your preferred IDE (IntelliJ IDEA, Eclipse, or Visual Studio Code), import the project, and you're ready to go!
- **Run the Application**: You'll find a Main class annotated with @SpringBootApplication. This is the entry point of your application. You can run the class, and Spring Boot will start an embedded server (like Tomcat) and host your application.

```java
@SpringBootApplication
public class DemoApplication {

    public static void main(String[] args) {
        SpringApplication.run(DemoApplication.class, args);
    }
}
```

Conclusion

Spring Boot removes much of the boilerplate and setup that previously made Spring projects complex to manage. With its auto-configuration, embedded servers, and microservices-friendly features, it empowers developers to create production-ready applications faster and with less code. Whether you're building a simple web app or a complex microservices architecture, Spring Boot has everything you need to get up and running quickly.

So, what's next? Now that you know the basics, you can dive deeper into building your first Spring Boot application, starting with a RESTful API, which is often the first step in modern web application development.

CHAPTER 2

SETTING UP A SPRING BOOT PROJECT

In this chapter, we will continue our Spring Boot journey with:

1. Learn more about the Spring Boot set-up
2. Spring Boot project structure
3. Understand the basic starter dependencies
4. Create a basic REST endpoint
5. Run and test the application

I use IntelliJ Idea as the IDE but you can use any IDE of your choice as it doesn't make any difference.

Now, let's set up a project!

Step 1: Using Spring Initializr

We have seen this step in the last article also. We will discuss this in detail here. This is the easiest way to create a Spring Boot project. This tool provides a user-friendly web interface that allows you to generate a basic Spring Boot project with your chosen dependencies.

1. Open Spring Initializr

Navigate to start.spring.io. This is the official Spring Initializr page where you can configure your project.

2. Configure Project Settings

- **Project Type**: Select Maven (or Gradle if you prefer).
- **Language**: Choose Java (Kotlin and Groovy are also supported).

Spring Boot Version: Use the stable latest version, which will be pre-selected for you.

- **Group and Artifact**: Enter values for the Group (typically a reverse domain like com.example) and Artifact (the name of your project). This artifact will be the jar name if not instructed otherwise. Try to give values that are relevant to your application. If you are creating an application for your employer or client try to give the client domain in group and artifact as the service name. Package name will change accordingly.

- **Packaging**: Choose between JAR and WAR packaging. For most applications, JAR is sufficient as it will run as a standalone service and is ideal for microservices or any web service.

3. Select Dependencies

Now, choose the dependencies you'll need for your project. For example:

- Spring Web: If you're building a web application or REST API.
- Spring Data JPA: For database interaction using JPA.
- Spring Security: If you plan to secure your application.

For a simple starter project, the Spring Web dependency is enough.

4. Generate the Project

Once everything is configured, click **Generate** to download the project as a zip file. Extract it to a directory on your local machine.

Step 2: Import the Project into Your IDE

Next, we'll import the downloaded project into your favourite Integrated Development Environment (IDE). Popular options include IntelliJ IDEA, Eclipse, or Visual Studio Code. I have used the IntelliJ community edition which is free to download and is enough for basic development.

1. Open Your IDE

- If you're using **IntelliJ IDEA**, choose File > Open and select the project folder.
- For **Eclipse**, use File > Import and select Existing Maven Projects.

2. Wait for Maven to Resolve Dependencies

When you open the project, your IDE will automatically download the necessary Maven dependencies (like Spring Boot, Spring Web, etc.) from the internet. This may take a few minutes.

Step 3: Understanding the Project Structure

Once the project is loaded in your IDE, take a moment to familiarize yourself with the default structure that Spring Boot creates:

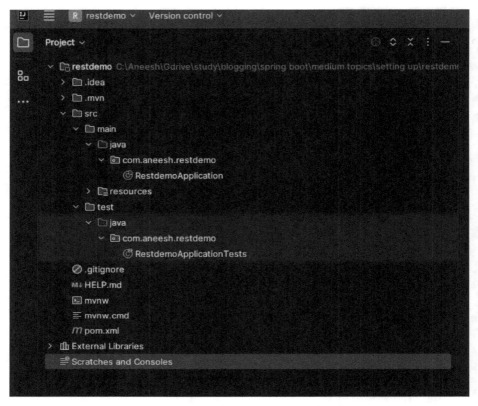

- **src/main/java**: This is where your Java code resides.
- **Application class**: Inside this directory, you'll find a class (usually named after your artifact) annotated with @SpringBootApplication. This class contains the main method, which is the entry point of your application.

```java
package com.aneesh.restdemo;

import org.springframework.boot.SpringApplication;
import org.springframework.boot.autoconfigure.SpringBootApplication;

@SpringBootApplication
public class RestdemoApplication {

  public static void main(String[] args) {
    SpringApplication.run(RestdemoApplication.class, args);
  }
}
```

- **src/main/resources**: Contains configuration files like application.properties or application.yml, where you'll define application settings like database connection or logging levels.

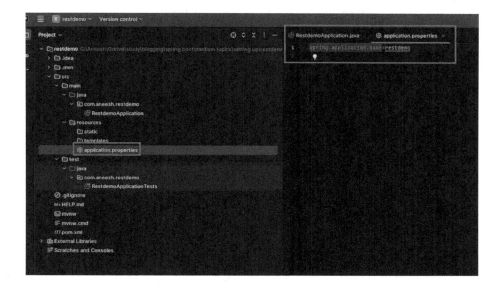

- **pom.xml:** This is the Maven build file. I have used Maven here but you can select any other build tool as well. It lists all the dependencies and configurations for your project. If you need to add more libraries later, you'll do it here.

Step 4: Running Your Spring Boot Application

Now that the project is set up, it's time to run your application!

1. Run the Application from the IDE

Find the main method inside the class annotated with @SpringBootApplication. In most IDEs, you can right-click this class and select Run.

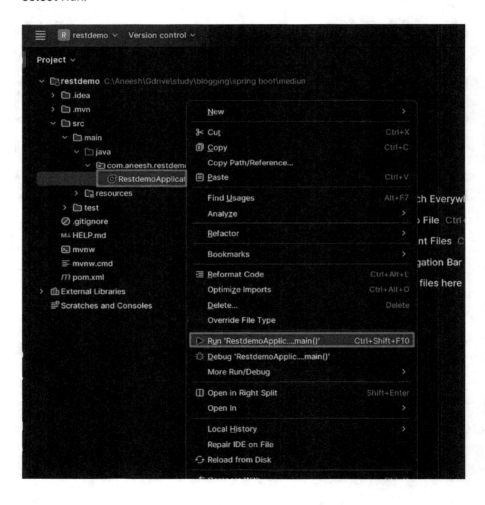

Once the application starts, you'll see logs indicating that the embedded Tomcat server has started, and the application is running on port 8080 by default.

2. Access the Application

Open a browser and go to http://localhost:8080. Since we haven't added any endpoints yet, you'll probably get a 404 Not Found response, but this confirms that your server is running!

Step 5: Adding a Simple REST Controller

Let's add a basic REST endpoint to verify that your Spring Boot application is up and running.

1. Create a Controller Class

Inside the src/main/java folder, create a new Java class named HelloController inside *com.aneesh.restdemo.controller* package

```java
package com.aneesh.restdemo.controller;

import org.springframework.web.bind.annotation.GetMapping;
import org.springframework.web.bind.annotation.RestController;

@RestController
public class HelloController {

    @GetMapping("/hello")
    public String sayHello() {
        return "Hello, Spring Boot!";
    }
}
```

- **@RestController**: Tells Spring that this class will handle HTTP requests.
- **@GetMapping("/hello")**: Maps the /hello URL to this method.
- **sayHello()**: This method will return a simple message when accessed.

2. Restart the Application

Save the file and restart your application. You can stop the application in the IDE and run it again.

3. Test the Endpoint

Open a browser and go to http://localhost:8080/hello. You should see the message "Hello, Spring Boot!".

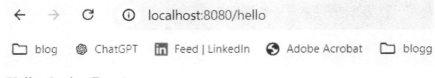

Hello, Spring Boot!

Step 6: Customize Application Properties

Spring Boot's application.properties file allows you to configure various settings for your project, like server ports or database connections. For example, to change the default port from 8080 to 9090, add the following line to src/main/resources/application.properties:

```
spring.application.name=restdemo
server.port=9090
```

Now when you restart your application, it will run on http://localhost:9090.

That's it! You have created a basic REST service within 5 minutes.

Conclusion

Setting up a Spring Boot project is incredibly simple, thanks to tools like Spring Initializr and Maven. With just a few steps, you can have a fully functional, ready-to-run application with minimal configuration. From here, you can start building RESTful APIs, connecting to databases, or adding security features — Spring Boot has all the tools to make your development process faster and easier.

This is just the start of your Spring Boot journey. In future articles, we'll explore how to create more complex APIs, integrate databases, secure your application, and many more. Stay tuned!

CHAPTER 3

SPRING BOOT ANNOTATIONS

By using annotations, Spring Boot eliminates much of the boilerplate code and complex configurations which was the way in traditional Java development. In this chapter, we'll dive into the most important Spring Boot annotations, explain their purpose, and show you how they simplify your application development.

What are Annotations in Spring Boot?

In Spring Boot, annotations provide metadata about a program's structure or behavior. Instead of writing lengthy XML configuration files, Spring Boot allows you to define behavior and logic with annotations directly in the code. For example, instead of manually configuring beans, controllers, or services in an external file, you can use annotations like @Component or @RestController to achieve the same result. This reduces the development effort and enhances code readability.

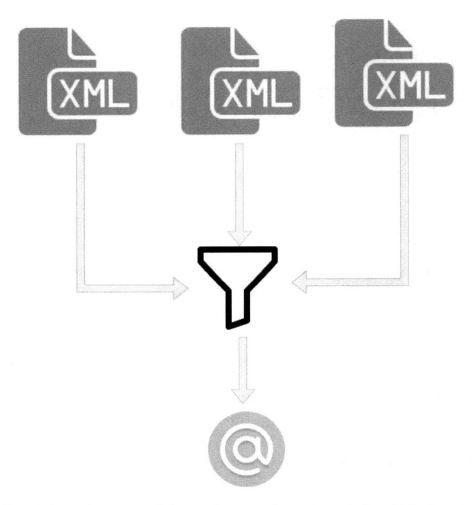

Now, let's explore some of the most commonly used annotations in Spring Boot and how they help in application development.

1. @SpringBootApplication

The @SpringBootApplication annotation is a core part of Spring Boot that is used on the main class which is the entry point of the application. This annotation essentially combines three other annotations: @Configuration, @EnableAutoConfiguration, and @ComponentScan.

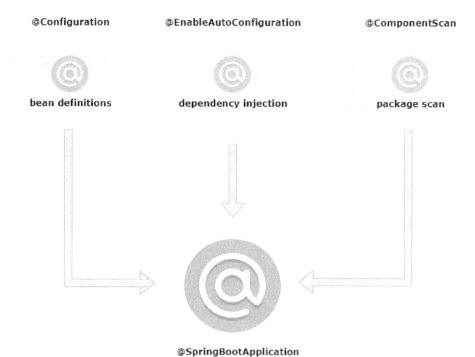

@Configuration   @EnableAutoConfiguration   @ComponentScan

bean definitions   dependency injection   package scan

@SpringBootApplication

Let's break them down:

- **@Configuration**: Marks the class as a source of bean definitions.
- **@EnableAutoConfiguration**: Enables Spring Boot's auto-configuration mechanism, which automatically sets up beans based on the dependencies in your project. For example, if Class B is a dependency for Class A then Spring Boot creates a bean for Class B and injects it into Class A before creating a Class A bean.
- **@ComponentScan**: Tells Spring to scan the project for components like controllers, services, and repositories. Here you can specify the base packages that Spring Boot needs to scan for bean creations.

Here's an example:

```
@SpringBootApplication
public class MyApplication {

    public static void main(String[] args) {
        SpringApplication.run(MyApplication.class, args);
    }
}
```

This single annotation enables Spring Boot to configure your application without manual setup.

2. @RestController

In a Spring Boot web application, the @RestController annotation is essential for creating RESTful web services. It is a specialization of, but it automatically adds @ResponseBody to the class, meaning that each method within the class returns the response body directly (typically JSON or XML).

```
@RestController
public class HelloController {
    @GetMapping("/hello")
    public String sayHello() {
        return "Hello, Spring Boot!";
    }
}
```

In this example, the @RestController annotation tells Spring Boot that this class will handle HTTP requests. The @GetMapping annotation maps the /hello endpoint to the sayHello() method

3. @RequestMapping, @GetMapping, and Other HTTP Mapping Annotations

Spring Boot provides several annotations for mapping HTTP requests to methods within a controller. These annotations are part of the Spring MVC framework:

- **@RequestMapping**: General-purpose annotation for mapping any HTTP request (GET, POST, PUT, DELETE) to a controller method.
- **@GetMapping**: Shorthand for @RequestMapping(method = RequestMethod.GET), used to map GET requests.
- **@PostMapping**: Used to handle POST requests.
- **@PutMapping**: Used for PUT requests.
- **@DeleteMapping**: Used to handle DELETE requests.

```java
@RestController
@RequestMapping("/api")
public class ApiController {

  @GetMapping("/users")
  public List<String> getUsers() {
    return List.of("John", "Jane", "Mike");
  }

  @PostMapping("/users")
  public String createUser(@RequestBody String user) {
    return "User created: " + user;
  }
}
```

In this case, @RequestMapping("/api") is applied at the class level, so all methods within this class are prefixed with /api. The @GetMapping and @PostMapping annotations map HTTP GET and POST requests respectively.

4. @Autowired

The @Autowired annotation allows Spring Boot to automatically inject dependencies. It is used to mark a constructor, method, or field as a point where Spring should inject a bean. Instead of manually wiring components together, Spring Boot handles this for you.

Example:

```java
@Service
public class UserService {

    private final UserRepository userRepository;

    @Autowired
    public UserService(UserRepository userRepository) {
        this.userRepository = userRepository;
    }
    public List<User> getAllUsers() {
        return userRepository.findAll();
    }
}
```

Here, the @Autowired annotation injects an instance of UserRepository into UserService. Spring Boot handles the creation and management of this bean, so you don't need to instantiate it manually.

Apart from @Autowired annotation, there are other ways like constructor and setter injection in the recent Spring Boot version to inject dependencies. We will discuss that in detail in upcoming articles

5. @Component, @Service, @Repository
These annotations are used to declare Spring-managed components, which can then be injected elsewhere in the application.

- @Component: A generic stereotype for any Spring-managed component.
- @Service: A specialized @Component, used for service-layer classes. It clarifies the intention that this class holds business logic.
- @Repository: Another specialization of @Component, used for data access objects (DAOs). It provides additional benefits like exception translation for database errors.

Example:

```
@Component
public class EmailSender {
  public void sendEmail(String message) {
    System.out.println("Sending email: " + message);
  }
}
@Service
public class NotificationService {
  private final EmailSender emailSender;
  @Autowired
  public NotificationService(EmailSender emailSender) {
  this.emailSender = emailSender;
  }
  public void notifyUser(String message) {
  emailSender.sendEmail(message);
  }
}
```

In this example, EmailSender is a generic Spring-managed component, while NotificationService is marked with @Service, making its role in the application more clear.

6. @Configuration and @Bean

The @Configuration annotation is used to mark a class as a source of bean definitions. Methods within this class that are annotated with @Bean define beans that Spring will manage.

Example:

```
@Configuration
public class AppConfig {

    @Bean
    public EmailSender emailSender() {
        return new EmailSender();
    }
}
```

In this case, the AppConfig class is annotated with @Configuration, and the emailSender() method is annotated with @Bean, meaning that Spring will manage the lifecycle of the EmailSender bean.

7. @EnableAutoConfiguration

This annotation is part of @SpringBootApplication, but it can also be used independently. It tells Spring Boot to automatically configure the application based on the dependencies included in the classpath.

For example, if you add spring-boot-starter-data-jpa to your dependencies, @EnableAutoConfiguration will automatically configure JPA and Hibernate without any manual setup.

8. @PathVariable and @RequestParam

These annotations help capture input from the URL and query parameters.

- **@PathVariable**: Extracts values from the URI path.
- **@RequestParam**: Extracts query parameters from the URL.

Example:

```
@GetMapping("/user/{id}")
public String getUserById(@PathVariable Long id) {
    return "User ID: " + id;
}

@GetMapping("/search")
public String searchUser(@RequestParam String name) {
    return "Searching for user: " + name;
}
```

Conclusion

Annotations are the backbone of Spring Boot's simplicity and flexibility. With just a few lines of annotated code, you can automate many complex tasks like dependency injection, HTTP request mapping, and bean management. As you explore Spring Boot further, you'll find that these annotations save time and help you write cleaner, more maintainable code.

By understanding these key Spring Boot annotations, you're well on your way to mastering Spring Boot development. Stay tuned for future articles where we explore advanced Spring Boot concepts!

CHAPTER 4

BUILDING A REST API WITH SPRING BOOT AND H2 DATABASE

Spring Boot makes building REST APIs easy, and you can quickly prototype, test, and build functional applications. In this chapter, we'll create a simple REST API using Spring Boot, with a persistent User resource stored in an H2 database. H2 is an in-memory database that doesn't require any software installation. Spring Boot itself creates an h2 database in the app memory when run. We'll use examples to explore each HTTP method (GET, POST, PUT, DELETE).

Prerequisites

Before you begin, make sure you have the following installed:
- **Java JDK** (version 8 or higher). You can download it from <u>here</u>.
- **Spring Boot** (via <u>Spring Initializr</u> or an IDE like <u>IntelliJ IDEA</u> or <u>Eclipse</u>)
- **Maven** (Spring Boot will manage dependencies automatically). You can follow this <u>article</u> to learn more about Maven

Step 1: Setting Up the Spring Boot Project

<u>You can set it up by following my chapter 2 on Spring Boot setup.</u>

Step 2: Configuring the H2 Database

By default, **Spring Boot** configures H2 as an in-memory database. We can make it persistent by adding the following lines to the application.properties file:

```
# Enable H2 console
spring.h2.console.enabled=true
spring.h2.console.path=/h2-console
# H2 database configuration
spring.datasource.url=jdbc:h2:mem:testdb
spring.datasource.driverClassName=org.h2.Driver
spring.datasource.username=sa
spring.datasource.password=password
spring.jpa.database-platform=org.hibernate.dialect.H2Dialect
spring.jpa.show-sql=true
spring.jpa.hibernate.ddl-auto=update
```

Example:

You can now access the H2 console at http://localhost:8080/h2-console and run SQL queries directly from the browser if you run the application.

Step 3: Creating the User Entity

We'll create a User entity stored in the H2 database.

```
@Entity
public class User {
  @Id
  @GeneratedValue(strategy = GenerationType.AUTO)
  private Long id;

  private String name;

  private String email;

  // Constructors, Getters, Setters
  public User() {}
```

```
public User(String name, String email) {
    this.name = name;
    this.email = email;
}

public Long getId() {
    return id;
}

public void setId(Long id) {
    this.id = id;
}

public String getName() {
    return name;
}

public void setName(String name) {
    this.name = name;
}

public String getEmail() {
    return email;
}

public void setEmail(String email) {
    this.email = email;
}
}
```

Step 4: Creating the User Repository

Next, we'll create a repository interface to interact with the database using Spring Data JPA.

```
import org.springframework.data.jpa.repository.JpaRepository;

public interface UserRepository extends JpaRepository<User, Long> {
}
```

This interface provides CRUD operations out of the box, like findAll(), save(), findById(), and deleteById().

Step 5: Creating the REST Controller

Now, we'll build the REST API to handle different HTTP methods.

1. GET Method: Retrieve All Users

We'll start by creating a method to retrieve all users.

```java
import org.springframework.beans.factory.annotation.Autowired;
import org.springframework.web.bind.annotation.GetMapping;
import org.springframework.web.bind.annotation.RequestMapping;
import org.springframework.web.bind.annotation.RestController;
import java.util.List;

@RestController
@RequestMapping("/api/users")
public class UserController {
    @Autowired
    private UserRepository userRepository;

    @GetMapping
    public List<User> getAllUsers() {
        return userRepository.findAll();
    }
}
```

Explanation:

- **@RestController:** Marks this class as a REST controller.
- **@RequestMapping("/api/users"):** Maps this controller to handle requests to /api/users.
- **@GetMapping:** Handles GET requests to retrieve all users from the database.

Test the GET Endpoint:

Navigate to http://localhost:8080/api/users in your browser or use Postman.
Since we haven't added any users yet, it will return an empty list:

[]

2. POST Method: Create a New User
Next, we'll create a method to add a new user to the database.

```java
import org.springframework.web.bind.annotation.PostMapping;
import org.springframework.web.bind.annotation.RequestBody;

@RestController
@RequestMapping("/api/users")
public class UserController {
    @Autowired
    private UserRepository userRepository;

    @PostMapping
    public User createUser(@RequestBody User user) {
        return userRepository.save(user);
    }
}
```

Explanation:

- **@PostMapping**: Maps POST requests to create a new user.
- **@RequestBody**: Converts the incoming JSON body to a User object.

Test the POST Endpoint:

Send a POST request to http://localhost:8080/api/users with the following
JSON body:

```json
{
  "name": "John Doe",
  "email": "john@example.com"
}
```

The response will be the created user with an auto-generated ID:

```json
{
  "id": 1,
  "name": "John Doe",
  "email": "john@example.com"
}
```

3. GET by ID Method: Retrieve a Single User

Now, let's create a method to retrieve a specific user by their ID.

```java
@RestController
@RequestMapping("/api/users")
public class UserController {

  @Autowired
  private UserRepository userRepository;
  @GetMapping("/{id}")
  public Optional<User> getUserById(@PathVariable Long id) {
    return userRepository.findById(id);
  }
}
```

Explanation:

- **@PathVariable:** Binds the {id} path variable to the method parameter.
- **findById():** Finds a user by their ID using Spring Data JPA.

Test the GET by ID Endpoint:

Navigate to http://localhost:8080/api/users/1. If the user with ID 1 exists, the response will be:

```
{
  "id": 1,
  "name": "John Doe",
  "email": "john@example.com"
}
```

4. PUT Method: Update an Existing User

To update an existing user, we'll use the PUT method.

```
@RestController
@RequestMapping("/api/users")
public class UserController {

  @Autowired
  private UserRepository userRepository;

  @PutMapping("/{id}")
  public User updateUser(@PathVariable Long id, @RequestBody User userDetails) {
    User user = userRepository.findById(id).orElseThrow();
    user.setName(userDetails.getName());
    user.setEmail(userDetails.getEmail());
    return userRepository.save(user);
  }
}
```

Explanation:

- **PUT**: Updates a user if they exist, otherwise throws an exception.
- **setName()** and **setEmail()**: Updates the user's details.

Test the PUT by ID Endpoint:

Send a PUT request to http://localhost:8080/api/users/1 with the following body:

```
{
"name": "Johnathan Doe",
"email": "johnathan@example.com"
}
```

The response will be:

```
{
"id": 1,
"name": "Johnathan Doe",
"email": "johnathan@example.com"
}
```

5. DELETE Method: Remove a User

Finally, we'll implement the DELETE method to remove a user by their ID.

```
@RestController
@RequestMapping("/api/users")
public class UserController {
  @Autowired
  private UserRepository userRepository;

  @DeleteMapping("/{id}")
  public String deleteUser(@PathVariable Long id) {
    userRepository.deleteById(id);
    return "User deleted with ID: " + id;
  }
}
```

Explanation:

- **@DeleteMapping**: Handles DELETE requests to remove a user from the database.
- **deleteById()**: Deletes a user based on their ID.

Test the DELETE Endpoint:

Send a DELETE request to http://localhost:8080/api/users/1. The response will be:

"User deleted with ID: 1"

Conclusion

In this guide, we built a complete REST API using Spring Boot and the H2 in-memory database, with a User entity as the resource. We explored various HTTP methods like GET, POST, PUT, and DELETE, each demonstrated with practical examples.

Spring Boot, combined with Spring Data JPA and H2, simplifies database operations and allows developers to focus on business logic rather than configuration. If you are using any other DB, then you just need to provide the relevant configuration in application.properties

With these basics in place, you can expand the API by adding features such as input validation, error handling, authentication, and more complex relationships between entities which we will discuss in upcoming articles.

So stay tuned and Happy coding!

CHAPTER 5

DEPENDENCY INJECTION AND INVERSION OF CONTROL (IOC)

In this chapter, we'll break down both concepts with easy-to-understand explanations and practical code examples. Let's get started!

What is Dependency Injection (DI)?

Dependency Injection is a design pattern where an object's dependencies (e.g., other objects it needs to work) are provided externally rather than the object creating them itself. In simple terms, instead of creating the objects manually inside the class, we **inject** them from the outside. This results in loosely coupled code and makes testing easier. Explaining in simple terms, if Class B is a member of Class A, then the Spring IoC container will analyze Class A , create Class B instance, and inject it into Class A while creating its instance.

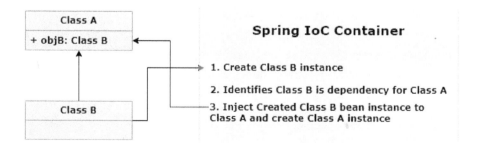

Think of it like ordering food at a restaurant: instead of cooking your own meal, you let the restaurant provide it for you.

Why use Dependency Injection?

- **Loose coupling:** Objects are no longer responsible for creating their dependencies, making the code flexible.
- **Testability:** Dependencies can be easily mocked or replaced for unit testing.
- **Maintainability:** Modifications to one class won't directly affect others.

What is Inversion of Control (IoC)?

Inversion of Control (IoC) is a principle where the control of objects or the flow of a program is inverted. Instead of the object controlling the dependencies (e.g., creating them or managing them), Spring (or another framework) takes control and manages the object lifecycle.

Think of it like hiring a service where someone else manages all the tasks for you rather than you doing them yourself.

Spring implements IoC using the Spring IoC Container. This container creates and manages the objects (beans) in the application and injects dependencies as needed.

Dependency Injection in Spring Boot

In Spring Boot, apart from @Autowired annotation which we discussed in the last article, DI is primarily achieved using **constructor injection** or **setter injection**. Let's explore both approaches.

1. Constructor-Based Dependency Injection

Constructor injection is the preferred method of DI in Spring. The dependencies are provided to the class via its constructor. Spring Boot will automatically inject these dependencies when the class is instantiated.

Example:

Let's assume we have a simple service that greets users.

```
public interface GreetingService {
    String greet(String name);
}
```

Now, let's create an implementation of this service:

```java
import org.springframework.stereotype.Service;

@Service
public class SimpleGreetingService implements GreetingService {
  @Override
  public String greet(String name) {
    return "Hello, " + name + "!";
  }
}
```

The @Service annotation tells Spring that this class should be treated as a bean (a managed object in the IoC container).

Next, we have a GreetingController that depends on GreetingService:

```java
@RestController
public class GreetingController {

  private final GreetingService greetingService;

  // Constructor-based injection
  public GreetingController(GreetingService greetingService) {
    this.greetingService = greetingService;
  }

  @GetMapping("/greet")
  public String greet(@RequestParam String name) {
    return greetingService.greet(name);
  }
}
```

Explanation:

- **Constructor-based injection**: The GreetingService is injected via the constructor. Spring automatically provides the SimpleGreetingService implementation when the GreetingController is created.
- The @RestController annotation indicates this class handles web requests, and the /greet endpoint takes a name as a query parameter.

Testing the endpoint:

When you hit http://localhost:8080/greet?name=John, the response will be:

```
Hello, John!
```

Spring Boot manages the lifecycle and injection of the GreetingService automatically, following the DI pattern.

2. Setter-Based Dependency Injection

In setter-based DI, Spring injects the dependencies through setter methods. This method is less preferred but useful when the dependencies are optional or when you want to change them later.

Example:

We'll modify the previous example to use setter injection:

```java
@RestController
public class GreetingController {

    private GreetingService greetingService;

    // Setter-based injection
    public void setGreetingService(GreetingService greetingService) {
        this.greetingService = greetingService;
    }

    @GetMapping("/greet")
    public String greet(@RequestParam String name) {
        return greetingService.greet(name);
    }
}
```

In this example, the GreetingService is injected through a setter method rather than the constructor.

When to use setter injection:
- When dependencies are **optional**.
- When you may want to change the dependency during the object's lifecycle.

Inversion of Control in Spring Boot

As mentioned, IoC is the concept of letting the framework (in this case, Spring) manage the object creation, configuration, and lifecycle. Spring's IoC Container does this by:

1. Scanning for components (classes annotated with @Service, @Controller, @Repository, etc.).
2. Automatically managing dependencies between these components by injecting the required objects where needed.

IoC in Action:

In the example above, when Spring Boot starts, it:

- Automatically creates an instance of SimpleGreetingService because it's marked with @Service.
- Identifies that GreetingController needs a GreetingService via constructor or setter.
- Injects the SimpleGreetingService instance into the GreetingController.

Benefits of Dependency Injection and IoC in Spring Boot

- Loose Coupling: Components are less dependent on each other, making the code more modular and maintainable.
- Easier Testing: Dependencies can be mocked or replaced during unit testing without modifying the core logic.
- Better Maintenance: Changes to one part of the system don't cascade to others, reducing the chance of bugs.
- Cleaner Code: You no longer need to worry about manually creating or managing objects, allowing you to focus on business logic.

A Practical Example with Multiple Services

Let's extend the example by adding another greeting service:

```java
import org.springframework.stereotype.Service;

@Service
public class FormalGreetingService implements GreetingService {
    @Override
    public String greet(String name) {
        return "Good day, " + name + ".";
    }
}
```

We now have two implementations of GreetingService:
SimpleGreetingService and FormalGreetingService.
To handle multiple implementations, we can use **qualifiers** in Spring to
specify which service we want to inject.

Example:

```java
import org.springframework.beans.factory.annotation.Qualifier;
import org.springframework.web.bind.annotation.GetMapping;
import org.springframework.web.bind.annotation.RequestParam;
import org.springframework.web.bind.annotation.RestController;

@RestController
public class GreetingController {

    private final GreetingService greetingService;

    public GreetingController(@Qualifier("formalGreetingService") GreetingService greetingService) {
        this.greetingService = greetingService;
    }
    @GetMapping("/greet")
    public String greet(@RequestParam String name) {
        return greetingService.greet(name);
    }
}
```

Explanation:

@Qualifier("formalGreetingService"): We use @Qualifier to tell Spring which
implementation to inject. In this case, the FormalGreetingService is injected.

Conclusion

In this chapter, we've explored **Dependency Injection** and **Inversion of Control** in Spring Boot. These concepts help decouple your code, making it easier to test, maintain, and scale.

We used:

- **Constructor-based DI** (preferred method).
- **Setter-based DI** (useful when dependencies are optional).
- **IoC in Spring** to manage the lifecycle and injection of objects automatically.

By leveraging these powerful concepts in Spring Boot, you can build applications that are flexible, maintainable, and robust. As you progress, you'll encounter more complex scenarios where DI and IoC make your code cleaner and more efficient.

Stay tuned for more Spring Boot tutorials and happy coding!

CHAPTER 6

JPA AND HIBERNATE

In this chapter, we'll explore how to use **JPA (Java Persistence API)** and **Hibernate** in Spring Boot to handle database operations seamlessly. By the end, you'll understand how to map Java objects to database tables and perform CRUD operations efficiently.

What is JPA?

JPA (Java Persistence API) is a specification that defines how Java objects are mapped to relational databases. It provides a standardized way of persisting data in a database without needing to write boilerplate SQL queries.

JPA is just a specification, meaning it needs an implementation. This is where **Hibernate** comes into play.

What is Hibernate?

Hibernate is a popular JPA implementation. It handles the actual database interaction, converting your Java objects into database tables and vice versa. Hibernate simplifies the process of database access, so you don't have to write complex SQL statements manually.

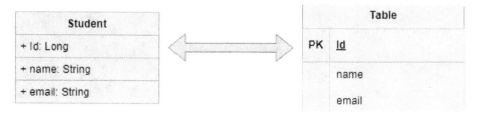

Step-by-Step Guide: Spring Boot with JPA and Hibernate

Let's walk through a basic example of using JPA and Hibernate in a Spring Boot application. We'll be working with a simple Student entity and performing CRUD (Create, Read, Update, Delete) operations on it.

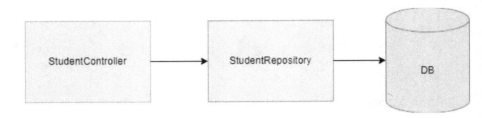

Step 1: Setting Up Your Project

1. Go to Spring Initializr.
2. Select **Maven** as the project type.
3. Add the following dependencies:
    - **Spring Data JPA**: For interacting with the database using JPA.
    - **H2 Database**: For an in-memory database (you can replace this with MySQL or PostgreSQL later).
    - **Spring Web**: To create REST endpoints.
4. Generate the project and open it in your IDE.

Step 2: Configuring the Database

First, let's configure the H2 in-memory database. Add the following lines to your application.properties file:

```
# H2 database configuration
spring.h2.console.enabled=true
spring.datasource.url=jdbc:h2:mem:testdb
spring.datasource.driverClassName=org.h2.Driver
spring.datasource.username=sa
spring.datasource.password=password
spring.jpa.database-platform=org.hibernate.dialect.H2Dialect
spring.jpa.hibernate.ddl-auto=update
```

These settings enable the H2 console, which allows you to access the database in your browser at http://localhost:8080/h2-console.

Step 3: Creating the Student Entity

An **entity** is a Java class that maps to a database table. In this example, we'll create a Student entity with fields like id, name, and email.

```java
import jakarta.persistence.Entity;
import jakarta.persistence.GeneratedValue;
import jakarta.persistence.GenerationType;
import jakarta.persistence.Id;

@Entity
public class Student {

    @Id
    @GeneratedValue(strategy = GenerationType.IDENTITY)
    private Long id;

    private String name;

    private String email;

    // Constructors
    public Student() {}

    public Student(String name, String email) {
        this.name = name;
        this.email = email;
    }
    // Getters and setters
    public Long getId() {
        return id;
    }

    public void setId(Long id) {
        this.id = id;
    }

    public String getName() {
        return name;
    }

    public void setName(String name) {
        this.name = name;
    }

    public String getEmail() {
        return email;
    }

    public void setEmail(String email) {
        this.email = email;
    }
}
```

Explanation

- **@Entity**: Marks the class as a JPA entity, which means it will be mapped to a database table.
- **@Id**: Defines the primary key for the entity.
- **@GeneratedValue**: Specifies that the ID will be automatically generated by the database.

Step 4: Creating the Student Repository

To interact with the database, we'll create a **repository** interface. Spring Data JPA provides a JpaRepository interface that offers methods for common database operations like save(), findById(), and deleteById().

```
import org.springframework.data.jpa.repository.JpaRepository;

public interface StudentRepository extends JpaRepository<Student, Long> {
}
```

Explanation:

- **JpaRepository<Student, Long>**: This interface manages the Student entity, with the primary key being of type Long.
- By extending JpaRepository, we automatically get several CRUD methods without writing any code.

Step 5: Creating a Student Controller

Now, we'll create a REST controller to expose endpoints for performing CRUD operations on the Student entity.

```java
import org.springframework.beans.factory.annotation.Autowired;
import org.springframework.web.bind.annotation.*;
import java.util.List;
import java.util.Optional;

@RestController
@RequestMapping("/api/students")
public class StudentController {

    @Autowired
    private StudentRepository studentRepository;

    // Get all students
    @GetMapping
    public List<Student> getAllStudents() {
        return studentRepository.findAll();
    }

    // Get a student by ID
    @GetMapping("/{id}")
    public Student getStudentById(@PathVariable Long id) {
        return studentRepository.findById(id).orElseThrow(() -> new RuntimeException("Student not found"));
    }

    // Create a new student
    @PostMapping
    public Student createStudent(@RequestBody Student student) {
        return studentRepository.save(student);
    }

    // Update a student
    @PutMapping("/{id}")
    public Student updateStudent(@PathVariable Long id, @RequestBody Student studentDetails) {
        Student student = studentRepository.findById(id).orElseThrow(() -> new RuntimeException("Student
not found"));
        student.setName(studentDetails.getName());
        student.setEmail(studentDetails.getEmail());
        return studentRepository.save(student);
    }

    // Delete a student
    @DeleteMapping("/{id}")
    public String deleteStudent(@PathVariable Long id) {
        studentRepository.deleteById(id);
        return "Student deleted successfully";
    }
}
```

Explanation:

- **@RestController**: Marks the class as a REST controller.
- **@RequestMapping("/api/students")**: Maps all the endpoints to /api/students.
- **studentRepository**: We inject the StudentRepository to interact with the database.

The various endpoints handle different CRUD operations:

- **GET** /api/students: Retrieves all students.
- **GET** /api/students/{id}: Retrieves a specific student by ID.
- **POST** /api/students: Creates a new student.
- **PUT** /api/students/{id}: Updates an existing student.
- **DELETE** /api/students/{id}: Deletes a student by ID.

Step 6: Testing the API

Now that the API is set up, you can test it using Postman, cURL, or directly from the browser.

1. Get All Students (GET /api/students):
Send a GET request to http://localhost:8080/api/students. Since no students have been created yet, this should return an empty list:

```
[ ]
```

2. Create a New Student (POST /api/students):
Send a POST request to http://localhost:8080/api/students with the following JSON body:

```
{
  "name": "Alice",
  "email": "alice@example.com"
}
```

The response will be:

```
{
  "id": 1,
  "name": "Alice",
  "email": "alice@example.com"
}
```

3. Get Student by ID (GET /api/students/1):

Now, send a GET request to http://localhost:8080/api/students/1 to retrieve the newly created student:

```
{
  "id": 1,
  "name": "Alice",
  "email": "alice@example.com"
}
```

4. Update a Student (PUT /api/students/1):

To update Alice's name, send a PUT request to http://localhost:8080/api/students/1 with the updated data:

```
{
  "name": "Alice Johnson",
  "email": "alice@example.com"
}
```

The response will be:

```
{
  "id": 1,
  "name": "Alice",
  "email": "alice@example.com"
}
```

5. Delete a Student (DELETE /api/students/1):

Finally, to delete the student, send a DELETE request to http://localhost:8080/api/students/1. The response will be:

```
"Student deleted successfully"
```

Conclusion

Congratulations! You've now created a complete CRUD API using **Spring Boot**, **JPA**, and **Hibernate**. We covered:

- Configuring an in-memory H2 database.
- Creating a JPA entity and mapping it to a database table.
- Performing CRUD operations using a repository.
- Exposing these operations through a REST controller.

Understanding JPA and Hibernate is essential for any developer working with databases in Java. As you progress, you can explore more complex relationships, such as OneToMany or ManyToMany, and try integrating a real-world database like MySQL or PostgreSQL.

In the next chapter, we'll dive deeper into database relationships and how to map them using JPA in Spring Boot.

Stay tuned for more exciting tutorials!

CHAPTER 7

HANDLING EXCEPTIONS

Exception handling is an important part of any application development. When things go wrong, like invalid data input or unavailable data, your application should be able to respond gracefully to the client system. In this chapter, we will learn how to handle exceptions in Spring Boot, provide user-friendly error messages, and make sure our application remains robust.

Why Handle Exceptions in Spring Boot?

When you build a web application or REST APIs, there is always a chance that something unexpected will happen and your application won't work as expected:

1. A user or client system might request for a resource that doesn't exist
2. Database or downstream system is down
3. The input data is not as per expected format

In such cases, the application will throw an exception and if these are not handled properly, the user will see messages which are not user-friendly or human-readable. This will make your application difficult to use and also it will not look professional.

Exception handling if done properly ensures that:

1. Exceptions are handled gracefully
2. Users receive meaningful and human-readable messages as a response
3. Developers also can debug issues more effectively

Step-by-Step Guide to Handling Exceptions

In this chapter, we will use a simple Spring Boot Project to demonstrate exception handling. We will continue and build on the last article's Student example.

Step 1: Basic Exception Handling with Try-Catch

The most basic way to handle exceptions is with a traditional try-catch block. Let's modify the StudentController to handle exceptions for getting a student by ID.

```java
@GetMapping("/{id}")
public Student getStudentById(@PathVariable Long id) {
  try {
    return studentRepository.findById(id)
    .orElseThrow(() -> new RuntimeException("Student not found"));
  } catch (RuntimeException ex) {
    System.out.println("Exception caught: " + ex.getMessage());
    return null;
  }
}
```

Explanation:

- We used try catch to handle any RuntimeException. If a student is not found, we throw an exception and catch it in the same method.
- This approach works, but it's not ideal for larger applications. It doesn't provide consistent error messages, and handling exceptions for every endpoint will lead to duplicated code.

Step 2: Handling Exceptions with @ExceptionHandler

Spring Boot provides the @ExceptionHandler annotation, which allows you to define a method that will handle exceptions globally or at a controller level.
Let's create a method to handle RuntimeException:

```
@RestController
@RequestMapping("/api/students")
public class StudentController {

    @Autowired
    private StudentRepository studentRepository;

    @GetMapping("/{id}")
    public Student getStudentById(@PathVariable Long id) {
      return studentRepository.findById(id)
        .orElseThrow(() -> new StudentNotFoundException("Student with ID " + id + " not found"));
    }

    // Exception handler for StudentNotFoundException
    @ExceptionHandler(StudentNotFoundException.class)
    public ResponseEntity<String> handleStudentNotFoundException(StudentNotFoundException ex) {
      return new ResponseEntity<>(ex.getMessage(), HttpStatus.NOT_FOUND);
    }
}
```

Explanation:

- We created a custom StudentNotFoundException to handle cases where a student isn't found in the database.
- The @ExceptionHandler annotation catches any StudentNotFoundExce and returns a meaningful error message along with an HTTP status code (404 Not Found)

Step 3: Creating a Global Exception Handler

Above Exception, handling is perfect if you just have one controller as its controller-level exception handler but in reality, you will have multiple Controller classes in your application. Hence instead of using a controller-level exception handler, we can use a global exception handler to manage all application exceptions at a single place.

Let's create a GlobalExceptionHandler class to handle exceptions across the application.

```
@ControllerAdvice
public class GlobalExceptionHandler {

    // Handle StudentNotFoundException globally
    @ExceptionHandler(StudentNotFoundException.class)
    public ResponseEntity<String> handleStudentNotFoundException(StudentNotFoundException ex) {
        return new ResponseEntity<>(ex.getMessage(), HttpStatus.NOT_FOUND);
    }

    // Handle generic exceptions globally
    @ExceptionHandler(Exception.class)
    public ResponseEntity<String> handleGenericException(Exception ex) {
        return new ResponseEntity<>("Something went wrong: " + ex.getMessage(),
HttpStatus.INTERNAL_SERVER_ERROR);
    }
}
```

Explanation:

- @ControllerAdvice: This annotation tells Spring that this class will handle exceptions globally for all controllers.
- @ExceptionHandler: We use this to handle specific exceptions, like StudentNotFoundException.
- We also created a method to handle any generic exceptions (Exception.class), returning a 500 Internal Server Error for unhandled exceptions.
- You can and should add more exception handlers based on different types of exceptions in your application.

Step 4: Customizing the Error Response

So far we have just returned a simple error message which is just a string. This might look ok but for a more robust application architecture, it might not be very informative for your API clients. It is always better to return a structured JSON response that includes not just a message but also additional details like timestamp and HTTP status. This is just an example you can add more additional details according to your application use case and your client.

We can create a custom error response object:

```java
import java.time.LocalDateTime;

public class ErrorResponse {

private LocalDateTime timestamp;

private String message;

private String details;

public ErrorResponse(LocalDateTime timestamp, String message, String details) {
  this.timestamp = timestamp;
  this.message = message;
  this.details = details;
}
// Getters and setters
}
```

Now, let's update our GlobalExceptionHandler to return this custom error response:

```java
import org.springframework.http.HttpStatus;
import org.springframework.http.ResponseEntity;
import org.springframework.web.bind.annotation.ControllerAdvice;
import org.springframework.web.bind.annotation.ExceptionHandler;
import java.time.LocalDateTime;

@ControllerAdvice
public class GlobalExceptionHandler {

@ExceptionHandler(StudentNotFoundException.class)
public ResponseEntity<ErrorResponse> handleStudentNotFoundException(StudentNotFoundException ex) {
  ErrorResponse errorResponse = new ErrorResponse(
  LocalDateTime.now(),
  ex.getMessage(),
  "Student resource not available"
  );
  return new ResponseEntity<>(errorResponse, HttpStatus.NOT_FOUND);
}

@ExceptionHandler(Exception.class)
public ResponseEntity<ErrorResponse> handleGenericException(Exception ex) {
  ErrorResponse errorResponse = new ErrorResponse(
  LocalDateTime.now(),
  "An unexpected error occurred",
  ex.getMessage()
  );
  return new ResponseEntity<>(errorResponse, HttpStatus.INTERNAL_SERVER_ERROR);
  }
}
```

Explanation:

- **ErrorResponse**: A simple POJO (Plain Old Java Object) to represent the error response in a structured format.
- **LocalDateTime.now()**: Captures the timestamp when the error occurred.
- The GlobalExceptionHandler now returns ErrorResponse objects instead of plain strings, providing more information about the error.

When a StudentNotFoundException is thrown, the response will look like this:

```json
{
"timestamp": "2024-09-24T10:15:30",
"message": "Student with ID 1 not found",
"details": "Student resource not available"
}
```

Step 5: Testing the Global Exception Handler

To test the exception handler, you can use a tool like **Postman** or **curl**.

1. Get a Non-Existing Student (GET /api/students/100): When you request a student that doesn't exist, the StudentNotFoundException will be thrown, and you'll receive a 404 Not Found response with a detailed error message:

```json
{
"timestamp": "2024-09-24T10:15:30",
"message": "Student with ID 100 not found",
"details": "Student resource not available"
}
```

2. Cause a Generic Error: You can deliberately cause an exception (like a null pointer) to see the 500 Internal Server Error response:

```
{
  "timestamp": "2024-09-24T10:15:30",
  "message": "An unexpected error occurred",
  "details": "NullPointerException"
}
```

Conclusion

You've now learned how to handle exceptions in a Spring Boot application, an essential skill for building robust APIs. We covered:

- **Basic exception handling** using try-catch.
- Using **@ExceptionHandler** to manage exceptions at the controller level.
- Creating a **GlobalExceptionHandler** to handle exceptions across the entire application.
- Returning a **custom error response** in JSON format to provide more context to users.

Mastering exception handling ensures that your applications are user-friendly and provide valuable feedback when something goes wrong. In the next article, we'll explore how to integrate Spring Boot with traditional databases like MySQL or PostgreSQL.

CHAPTER 8

SPRING BOOT WITH MYSQL AND POSTGRESQL

In this chapter, we're stepping up by connecting Spring Boot with **MySQL** and **PostgreSQL** — two of the most popular relational databases used in production environments.

By the end of this chapter, you will know how to:
1. Set up MySQL or PostgreSQL for a Spring Boot project.
2. Configure the database connection.
3. Perform basic CRUD operations using JPA.

Step 1: Setting Up MySQL or PostgreSQL

Installing MySQL

If you don't already have MySQL installed, you can download it from the MySQL official website. Follow the installation instructions for your operating system.
Once MySQL is installed, start the server and create a database for our Spring Boot application.

```
CREATE DATABASE springbootdb;
CREATE USER 'springuser'@'%' IDENTIFIED BY 'password';
GRANT ALL PRIVILEGES ON springbootdb.* TO 'springuser'@'%';
```

This creates a user springuser with a password password and grants it full privileges on the springbootdb database.

Installing PostgreSQL

Similarly, if you prefer to use PostgreSQL, you can download it from the PostgreSQL official website.

Once installed, create a database and user in PostgreSQL:

```
CREATE DATABASE springbootdb;
CREATE USER springuser WITH ENCRYPTED PASSWORD 'password';
GRANT ALL PRIVILEGES ON DATABASE springbootdb TO springuser;
```

Step 2: Adding MySQL/PostgreSQL Dependency

To connect Spring Boot with MySQL or PostgreSQL, we need to include the necessary dependencies in the pom.xml file.

For **MySQL**, add the following dependency:

```
<dependency>
<groupId>mysql</groupId>
<artifactId>mysql-connector-java</artifactId>
<scope>runtime</scope>
</dependency>
```

For **PostgreSQL**, add this:

```xml
<dependency>
<groupId>org.postgresql</groupId>
<artifactId>postgresql</artifactId>
<scope>runtime</scope>
</dependency>
```

Step 3: Configuring Application Properties

Now that we have the necessary dependencies, we need to configure the connection settings for MySQL or PostgreSQL in our application.properties or application.yml file. This is similar to what we did for H2 database only we need to change the driver class name for respective DB.

For MySQL, add the following in src/main/resources/application.properties:

```properties
spring.datasource.url=jdbc:mysql://localhost:3306/springbootdb
spring.datasource.username=springuser
spring.datasource.password=password
spring.datasource.driver-class-name=com.mysql.cj.jdbc.Driver
spring.jpa.hibernate.ddl-auto=update
spring.jpa.show-sql=true
```

For MySQL, add the following in src/main/resources/application.properties:

```
spring.datasource.url=jdbc:postgresql://localhost:5432/springbootdb
spring.datasource.username=springuser
spring.datasource.password=password
spring.datasource.driver-class-name=org.postgresql.Driver
spring.jpa.hibernate.ddl-auto=update
spring.jpa.show-sql=true
```

Explanation:

- spring.datasource.url: The JDBC URL for your database.
- spring.datasource.username and password: Credentials for connecting to the database.
- spring.jpa.hibernate.ddl-auto=update: Automatically updates the database schema when necessary.
- spring.jpa.show-sql=true: Enables SQL logging in the console (useful for debugging).

The rest of the steps are the same as what we followed in previous chapters where we created Student entity, repository, and controller classes. I am just putting these steps again here for this article to be a complete tutorial.

Step 4: Creating a JPA Entity

Let's create a Student entity that maps to a table in our **MySQL** or **PostgreSQL** database. This is again the same Student class that we used in previous articles. I am just mentioning this again here for the sake of this post's continuity.

```
@Entity
public class Student {
@Id
@GeneratedValue(strategy = GenerationType.IDENTITY)
private Long id;
private String name;
private String email;
```

```
// Getters and setters
public Long getId() {
return id;
}
public void setId(Long id) {
this.id = id;
}
public String getName() {
return name;
}
public void setName(String name) {
this.name = name;
}
public String getEmail() {
return email;
}
public void setEmail(String email) {
this.email = email;
}
}
```

Explanation:

- The @Entity annotation tells Spring Boot that this class represents a table in the database.
- @Id and @GeneratedValue annotate the primary key, which will be automatically generated.

Step 5: Creating a Repository

Next, create a repository interface to handle CRUD operations.

```
import org.springframework.data.jpa.repository.JpaRepository;
public interface StudentRepository extends JpaRepository<Student, Long> {
}
```

Explanation:

- **JpaRepository**: This interface provides built-in methods for basic CRUD operations (like save, findAll, findById, etc.).

Step 6: Creating REST Endpoints

Now, let's expose some REST endpoints to perform CRUD operations on the Student resource. We'll build a basic controller to handle HTTP requests.

```java
import org.springframework.beans.factory.annotation.Autowired;
import org.springframework.web.bind.annotation.*;
import java.util.List;

@RestController
@RequestMapping("/api/students")
public class StudentController {

    @Autowired
    private StudentRepository studentRepository;

    @GetMapping
    public List<Student> getAllStudents() {
        return studentRepository.findAll();
    }

    @PostMapping
    public Student createStudent(@RequestBody Student student) {
        return studentRepository.save(student);
    }

    @GetMapping("/{id}")
    public Student getStudentById(@PathVariable Long id) {
        return studentRepository.findById(id)
        .orElseThrow(() -> new RuntimeException("Student not found"));
    }

    @PutMapping("/{id}")
    public Student updateStudent(@PathVariable Long id, @RequestBody Student updatedStudent) {
        Student student = studentRepository.findById(id)
        .orElseThrow(() -> new RuntimeException("Student not found"));
        student.setName(updatedStudent.getName());
        student.setEmail(updatedStudent.getEmail());
        return studentRepository.save(student);
    }

    @DeleteMapping("/{id}")
    public void deleteStudent(@PathVariable Long id) {
        studentRepository.deleteById(id);
    }
}
```

Explanation:

- **@GetMapping**: Retrieves all students from the database.
- **@PostMapping**: Adds a new student.

- **@GetMapping("/{id}")**: Retrieves a student by ID.
- **@PutMapping("/{id}")**: Updates an existing student.
- **@DeleteMapping("/{id}")**: Deletes a student by ID.

Step 7: Testing the Application

To test the application, you can use a tool like Postman or curl.

1.Add a New Student (POST /api/students):

```
{
    "name": "John Doe",
    "email": "john.doe@example.com"
}
```

2. Get All Students (GET /api/students): This will return a list of all students.

3. Update a Student (PUT /api/students/{id}): You can update a student by providing the updated information.

4. Delete a Student (DELETE /api/students/{id}): Removes a student from the database.

Conclusion

In this chapter, we covered how to connect a Spring Boot application to **MySQL** or **PostgreSQL**, two of the most widely used databases in production. We walked through the process of setting up the database, configuring the application properties, and creating entities, repositories, and controllers to interact with the database.

This is a fundamental skill for any Java developer working with data-driven applications, and you're now well-equipped to work with relational databases in Spring Boot.

In the next chapter, we'll explore how to implement **security in Spring Boot**.

CHAPTER 9

SPRING BOOT SECURITY BASICS

In this chapter, we're diving into Spring Boot Security, which is crucial for any real-world application.

Spring Boot makes it easier to secure your application through a framework called Spring Security, which helps manage authentication, authorization, and protection against common security threats.

By the end of this article, you'll understand:

1. **The basics of Spring Boot Security.**
2. **How to secure endpoints.**
3. **The difference between authentication and authorization.**
4. **Roles and role-based access control (RBAC).**
5. **Configuring security in a Spring Boot application.**

Step 1: What is Spring Boot Security?

Spring Boot Security is an integrated part of the Spring framework that helps secure your application by:

- **Authenticating** users (verifying their identity).
- **Authorizing** users (deciding what users can and can't do).
- Protecting against **common attacks** like Cross-Site Scripting (XSS), Cross-Site Request Forgery (CSRF), and Session Hijacking.

Spring Security is highly customizable but offers many out-of-the-box features that can be used with minimal configuration. Let's break down its two core aspects: **authentication** and **authorization**.

Step 2: Authentication vs Authorization

- **Authentication:** The process of verifying who a user is. For example, when a user logs into an application using a username and password.
- **Authorization:** The process of deciding what an authenticated user can access. For example, users with the "ADMIN" role can access the admin panel, while users with the "USER" role cannot.

Step 3: Adding Spring Security to Your Project

To add Spring Security, include the following dependency, which is the starter dependency for Spring security, in your pom.xml:

```xml
<dependency>
    <groupId>org.springframework.boot</groupId>
    <artifactId>spring-boot-starter-security</artifactId>
</dependency>
```

Or if you are using **Gradle**:

```
implementation 'org.springframework.boot:spring-boot-starter-security'
```

Once you add this dependency, **Spring Security** will automatically secure all your endpoints by default, requiring authentication for all requests.

Step 4: Configuring Basic Security

By default, Spring Security uses form-based authentication and protects all URLs. Let's customize the configuration to suit our needs.

Create a new **SecurityConfig** class to configure your security settings:

```java
import org.springframework.context.annotation.Bean;
import org.springframework.security.config.annotation.web.builders.HttpSecurity;
import org.springframework.security.config.annotation.web.configuration.EnableWebSecurity;
import org.springframework.security.core.userdetails.User;
import org.springframework.security.core.userdetails.UserDetails;
import org.springframework.security.core.userdetails.UserDetailsService;
import org.springframework.security.provisioning.InMemoryUserDetailsManager;
import org.springframework.security.web.SecurityFilterChain;

@EnableWebSecurity
public class SecurityConfig {

    @Bean
    public SecurityFilterChain securityFilterChain(HttpSecurity http) throws Exception {
        http
        .authorizeHttpRequests((requests) -> requests
        .requestMatchers("/admin/**").hasRole("ADMIN")
        .requestMatchers("/user/**").hasAnyRole("USER", "ADMIN")
        .anyRequest().authenticated()
        )
        .formLogin((form) -> form
        .loginPage("/login")
        .permitAll()
        )
        .logout((logout) -> logout.permitAll());
        return http.build();
    }

    @Bean
    public UserDetailsService userDetailsService() {
        UserDetails user = User.withDefaultPasswordEncoder()
        .username("user")
        .password("password")
        .roles("USER")
        .build();

        UserDetails admin = User.withDefaultPasswordEncoder()
        .username("admin")
        .password("adminpassword")
        .roles("ADMIN")
        .build();
        return new InMemoryUserDetailsManager(user, admin);
    }
}
```

Explanation:

- **SecurityFilterChain**: This defines how requests should be handled.
- /admin/** is restricted to users with the "ADMIN" role.
- /user/** can be accessed by both "USER" and "ADMIN".
- All other requests require the user to be authenticated.
- **InMemoryUserDetailsManager**: This is a simple, in-memory store of users, useful for demonstration purposes. In a real application, you would connect this to a database by including JPA classes like repository and entity classes for the database table.
- **formLogin**: Enables form-based authentication with a default login page.

Step 5: Role-Based Access Control (RBAC)

Roles help in determining what actions a user can perform in the system. In our configuration, we have two roles:

- **USER**: Can access regular user pages.
- **ADMIN**: Can access both user and admin pages.

Spring Security checks for roles with **hasRole("ROLE_NAME")** or **hasAnyRole("ROLE1", "ROLE2")**.

```java
import org.springframework.web.bind.annotation.GetMapping;
import org.springframework.web.bind.annotation.RestController;

@RestController
public class HomeController {

  @GetMapping("/admin")
  public String admin() {
    return "Welcome, Admin!";
  }

  @GetMapping("/user")
  public String user() {
    return "Welcome, User!";
  }

  @GetMapping("/home")
  public String home() {
    return "Welcome to the home page!";
  }
}
```

Step 6: Testing the Application

Now, let's run the application and test it using the following steps:

1. Access the Home Page:
- Go to http://localhost:8080/home. You'll be redirected to the login page since the home endpoint requires authentication.

2. Login with User Credentials:
- Enter the credentials: username: user and password: password.
- After logging in, you can access the /user endpoint but will be denied access to /admin.

3. Login with Admin Credentials:
- Enter the credentials: username: admin and password: adminpassword.
- The admin can access both /user and /admin endpoints.

Step 7: Securing REST APIs with Spring Boot

You can also secure REST APIs using Spring Boot Security. In REST APIs, form-based login is not as common as token-based or HTTP Basic authentication.

Let's modify our security configuration to use **HTTP Basic Authentication**:

```
@Bean
public SecurityFilterChain securityFilterChain(HttpSecurity http) throws Exception {
    http
    .authorizeHttpRequests((requests) -> requests
    .requestMatchers("/api/admin/**").hasRole("ADMIN")
    .requestMatchers("/api/user/**").hasAnyRole("USER", "ADMIN")
    .anyRequest().authenticated()
    )
    .httpBasic(); // Use HTTP Basic Authentication
    return http.build();
}
```

With HTTP Basic Authentication, the client sends the username and password in the HTTP request header. This is often used in API calls.

Let's create a simple REST controller:

```java
@RestController
@RequestMapping("/api")
public class ApiController {

  @GetMapping("/admin")
  public String adminEndpoint() {
    return "Admin Access";
  }

  @GetMapping("/user")
  public String userEndpoint() {
    return "User Access";
  }
}
```

Step 8: Protecting Against Common Security Vulnerabilities

Spring Security also helps protect your application from common vulnerabilities:

1. **Cross-Site Request Forgery (CSRF)**: Prevents unauthorized actions on behalf of a logged-in user.
2. **Cross-Site Scripting (XSS)**: Blocks malicious scripts embedded in web pages.
3. **Session Hijacking**: Secures user sessions from being hijacked by attackers.

By default, Spring Security provides CSRF protection, but you may disable it for stateless APIs:

```
http.csrf().disable(); // Only for stateless APIs
```

Conclusion

In this article, we covered the basics of Spring Boot Security, focusing on:

- Authentication and Authorization.
- Setting up In-Memory Authentication with roles.
- Role-Based Access Control (RBAC).
- Securing REST APIs using HTTP Basic Authentication.
- Protecting against common security vulnerabilities.

Understanding Spring Security is crucial for building secure, production-ready applications. You now have a solid foundation to explore more advanced security features like JWT authentication, OAuth2, and custom security filters.

In the next chapter, we'll explore **Security with OAuth2 and JWT in Spring Boot**.

CHAPTER 10

ADVANCED SECURITY WITH OAUTH2 AND JWT

In this chapter, we will use **OAuth2** and **JWT (JSON Web Token)** to implement secure, token-based authentication in a Spring Boot application.

By the end of this article, you'll:
1. Understand the fundamentals of **OAuth2** and JWT.
2. Implement **OAuth2** with **JWT** in Spring Boot to secure RESTful APIs.
3. Build role-based access control using JWT scopes.
4. Step through real-world code examples to solidify your understanding.

Understanding OAuth2 and JWT

Before diving into the code, let's break down these two technologies:

OAuth2 (Open Authorization 2.0)

OAuth2 is an open standard that enables clients (like mobile or web applications) to obtain limited access to user resources without exposing their credentials. Instead of dealing with username-password combos, OAuth2 uses access tokens to handle authorization.

A typical OAuth2 flow:
1. The user logs into the application (the client).
2. The client requests permission from the user to access certain resources.
3. The authorization server grants an **access token** that the client uses to access protected resources.

JWT (JSON Web Token)

JWT is a compact, self-contained token format used to securely transmit information between parties as a JSON object. JWTs are commonly used in stateless authentication systems where each HTTP request carries its own authentication token.

A JWT consists of:
1. Header: Specifies the type of token and signing algorithm.
2. Payload: Contains claims (data) such as user roles or permissions.
3. Signature: Verifies the integrity of the token.

Setting Up the Environment

In this chapter, we will:
- Implement OAuth2 with JWT for authentication.
- We will continue and enhance our Student management API.
- Use H2 as an in-memory database for simplicity.

Let's begin by setting up our Spring Boot project.

Step 1: Adding Required Dependencies

Update your pom.xml to include OAuth2 and JWT dependencies.

```xml
<dependency>
<groupId>org.springframework.boot</groupId>
<artifactId>spring-boot-starter-oauth2-resource-server</artifactId>
</dependency>
<dependency>
<groupId>org.springframework.security</groupId>
<artifactId>spring-security-oauth2-jose</artifactId>
</dependency>
```

Or, if you're using Gradle:

```
implementation 'org.springframework.boot:spring-boot-starter-oauth2-resource-server'
implementation 'org.springframework.security:spring-security-oauth2-jose'
```

These dependencies allow us to configure Spring Boot as an OAuth2 resource server, capable of verifying JWTs for authorization.

Step 2: Creating a Basic Student Management API

Let's reuse our StudentController class from previous chapters.

```java
import org.springframework.web.bind.annotation.*;
import java.util.ArrayList;
import java.util.List;

@RestController
@RequestMapping("/api/students")
public class StudentController {
    private List<Student> students = new ArrayList<>();

    // Retrieve all students
    @GetMapping
    public List<Student> getAllStudents() {
        return students;
    }

    // Add a new student
    @PostMapping
    public String addStudent(@RequestBody Student student) {
        students.add(student);
        return "Student added successfully!";
    }

    // Update a student's information
    @PutMapping("/{id}")
    public String updateStudent(@PathVariable int id, @RequestBody Student updatedStudent) {
        students.set(id, updatedStudent);
        return "Student updated successfully!";
    }

    // Delete a student by ID
    @DeleteMapping("/{id}")
    public String deleteStudent(@PathVariable int id) {
        students.remove(id);
        return "Student deleted successfully!";
    }
}
```

The StudentController provides basic CRUD operations for managing students. Next, let's introduce security with OAuth2 and JWT.

Step 3: Configuring Spring Security with OAuth2

Now, let's configure Spring Boot as an OAuth2 resource server to accept and validate JWTs.

Security Configuration

```java
import org.springframework.context.annotation.Bean;
import org.springframework.security.config.annotation.web.builders.HttpSecurity;
import org.springframework.security.config.annotation.web.configuration.EnableWebSecurity;
import org.springframework.security.oauth2.server.resource.authentication.JwtAuthenticationConverter;
import org.springframework.security.oauth2.server.resource.authentication.JwtGrantedAuthoritiesConverter;
import org.springframework.security.web.SecurityFilterChain;

@EnableWebSecurity
public class SecurityConfig {
    @Bean
    public SecurityFilterChain securityFilterChain(HttpSecurity http) throws Exception {
        http
        .authorizeHttpRequests(authz -> authz
        .antMatchers("/api/students/**").hasAuthority("SCOPE_student.write")
        .anyRequest().authenticated()
        )
        .oauth2ResourceServer(oauth2 -> oauth2.jwt(jwt ->
jwt.jwtAuthenticationConverter(jwtAuthenticationConverter())));
        return http.build();
    }

    private JwtAuthenticationConverter jwtAuthenticationConverter() {
        JwtGrantedAuthoritiesConverter grantedAuthoritiesConverter = new JwtGrantedAuthoritiesConverter();
        grantedAuthoritiesConverter.setAuthorityPrefix("ROLE_");
        grantedAuthoritiesConverter.setAuthoritiesClaimName("scope");
        JwtAuthenticationConverter jwtAuthenticationConverter = new JwtAuthenticationConverter();
        jwtAuthenticationConverter.setJwtGrantedAuthoritiesConverter(grantedAuthoritiesConverter);
        return jwtAuthenticationConverter;
    }
}
```

Explanation:

- The **/api/students/**** endpoint is protected and only accessible to users with the **SCOPE_student.write** authority.
- The **JwtAuthenticationConverter** converts JWT scopes into Spring Security roles (ROLE_student.write), ensuring role-based access control.

Step 4: Integrating JWT and OAuth2 Using Keycloak

To keep things simple, we'll use Keycloak as our OAuth2 provider. Keycloak will issue JWTs, which our Spring Boot application will validate. Keycloak is the third-party Authorization server that provides the token based on the client.

Setting Up Keycloak:

1. Download and run Keycloak.
2. Create a realm named springboot.
3. Add a client (e.g., student-api-client) with **Bearer-Only** access.
4. Create roles such as student.read and student.write.
5. Assign these roles to a user.

Configuring Spring Boot for Keycloak:

Update application.yml to point to Keycloak's issuer URI.

```yaml
spring:
  security:
    oauth2:
      resourceserver:
        jwt:
          issuer-uri: http://localhost:8080/realms/springboot
```

This configuration ensures that Spring Boot will only accept JWT tokens issued by your Keycloak realm.

Step 5: Testing the API

Obtaining a JWT Token:

You can use Postman or cURL to request a JWT from Keycloak:

```
curl --location --request POST
'http://localhost:8080/realms/springboot/protocol/openid-connect/token' \
--header 'Content-Type: application/x-www-form-urlencoded' \
--data-urlencode 'client_id=student-api-client' \
--data-urlencode 'username=your-username' \
--data-urlencode 'password=your-password' \
--data-urlencode 'grant_type=password'
```

This will return a JWT token. Now you can use this token to access the Student API.

Testing with Postman:

- Set the Authorization header to Bearer <your-jwt-token>.
- Make a POST request to /api/students to add a new student.
- Make a GET request to retrieve the list of students.

Each request will be authorized based on the scopes in the JWT.

Step 6: Role-Based Authorization with JWT

In this example, we'll refine the authorization logic by separating read and write access based on the user's roles.

1. Users with the student.read scope can view student data.
2. Users with the student.write scope can add or modify student data.

Modify your SecurityConfig as follows:

```
http
    .authorizeHttpRequests(authz -> authz
        .antMatchers(HttpMethod.GET, "/api/students/**").hasAuthority("SCOPE_student.read")
        .antMatchers(HttpMethod.POST, "/api/students").hasAuthority("SCOPE_student.write")
        .anyRequest().authenticated()
    );
```

This ensures that only users with the SCOPE_student.read authority can view student records, while only those with SCOPE_student.write can modify them.

Conclusion

In this tutorial, you learned how to:

- Set up OAuth2 with JWT in a Spring Boot application.
- Secure a Student API with role-based access control using JWT.
- Implement OAuth2 with Keycloak as the authorization server.
- Configure Spring Security to manage and validate JWT tokens.

As modern applications grow, securing them with **OAuth2** and **JWT** is essential for both performance and scalability. This combination of technologies allows your application to securely manage user sessions and access across multiple devices and services.

CHAPTER 11

PAGINATION AND SORTING

Sorting is essential for presenting data in an organized way, whether it's in alphabetical order, by date, or based on other criteria.

In this chapter, we will:

1. Implement pagination and sorting in the Student API.
2. Utilize Spring Boot's Pageable and Sort features.
3. Explore practical examples with real-world code.

Step 1: Setting Up the Project

Let's begin by establishing the fundamentals. If you already have the Student API from our earlier chapters, we'll build upon that.

For those who are just starting, make sure you include the necessary dependencies in your pom.xml:

```xml
<dependency>
<groupId>org.springframework.boot</groupId>
<artifactId>spring-boot-starter-data-jpa</artifactId>
</dependency>
<dependency>
<groupId>com.h2database</groupId>
<artifactId>h2</artifactId>
<scope>runtime</scope>
</dependency>
```

These dependencies are needed for Spring Data JPA and H2 database (or another database if preferred).

Step 2: Create Student Entity and Repository

We'll use a simple Student entity that represents students in our database.

Student Entity:

```java
@Entity
public class Student {

@Id
@GeneratedValue(strategy = GenerationType.IDENTITY)
private Long id;

private String name;

private String email;

private String department;
// Getters and Setters
}
```

Student Repository:

We'll need a repository to interact with the database. The repository will extend JpaRepository, which comes with built-in methods for pagination and sorting.

```java
import org.springframework.data.jpa.repository.JpaRepository;

public interface StudentRepository extends JpaRepository<Student, Long> {
}
```

Step 3: Implementing Pagination and Sorting

Next, we will update the StudentController to incorporate pagination and sorting features. Spring Boot offers the Pageable and Sort classes, which simplify the implementation process.

Paginated and Sorted API in the Controller:

```java
import org.springframework.beans.factory.annotation.Autowired;
import org.springframework.data.domain.Page;
import org.springframework.data.domain.PageRequest;
import org.springframework.data.domain.Pageable;
import org.springframework.data.domain.Sort;
import org.springframework.web.bind.annotation.*;

@RestController
@RequestMapping("/api/students")
public class StudentController {

    @Autowired
    private StudentRepository studentRepository;

    // Get paginated and sorted students
    @GetMapping
    public Page<Student> getStudents(
            @RequestParam(defaultValue = "0") int page,
            @RequestParam(defaultValue = "5") int size,
            @RequestParam(defaultValue = "name") String sortBy) {

        Pageable pageable = PageRequest.of(page, size, Sort.by(sortBy));
        return studentRepository.findAll(pageable);
    }
}
```

Explanation:

The Pageable object is created with PageRequest.of(page, size, Sort.by(sortBy)), allowing you to define the page number, the number of records per page, and the sorting field.

- We then utilize the findAll(pageable) method from JpaRepository, which provides a Page object that includes the results.

This endpoint enables users to:

- Fetch students in pages.
- Organize the students based on the specified field (e.g., name, department, etc.).

Step 4: Testing the API

Let's test the API using **Postman** or **curl**.
- **URL**: /api/students
- **Method**: GET
- **Parameters**:

1. page: The page number (starting from 0).
2. size: The number of students per page.
3. sortBy: The field to sort by (default is "name").

Example 1: Fetching First Page, Sorted by Name

```
curl "http://localhost:8080/api/students?page=0&size=5&sortBy=name"
```

Response:

```json
{
    "content": [
        {
            "id": 1,
            "name": "Alice",
            "email": "alice@example.com",
            "department": "Computer Science"
        },
        // More students
    ],
    "totalPages": 2,
    "totalElements": 10,
    "size": 5,
    "number": 0
}
```

Example 1: Fetching First Page, Sorted by Name

```
curl "http://localhost:8080/api/students?page=1&size=5&sortBy=department"
```

This will retrieve the second page of students, sorted by the department field.

Step 5: Customizing the Pagination and Sorting Logic

In certain situations, you may need to sort by various criteria or enable sorting in both ascending and descending order. Spring offers extra flexibility to accommodate these needs.

Handling Multiple Sort Fields and Directions

We can adjust the controller to handle more advanced sorting options, like sorting by multiple fields or choosing the order (ascending or descending).

```java
@GetMapping
public Page<Student> getStudents(
        @RequestParam(defaultValue = "0") int page,
        @RequestParam(defaultValue = "5") int size,
        @RequestParam(defaultValue = "name") String[] sortBy,
        @RequestParam(defaultValue = "asc") String sortDirection) {

    Sort.Direction direction = sortDirection.equalsIgnoreCase("desc") ? Sort.Direction.DESC :
Sort.Direction.ASC;
    Pageable pageable = PageRequest.of(page, size, Sort.by(direction, sortBy));
    return studentRepository.findAll(pageable);
}
```

In this updated code:
- We introduced the capability to sort by multiple fields (for example, sortBy=name, department).
- You can now specify the sorting direction (either ascending or descending) using sortDirection.

Example : Fetching Students Sorted by Name and Department, in Descending Order

```bash
curl "http://localhost:8080/api/students?page=0&size=5&sortBy=name,department&sortDirection=desc"
```

This will retrieve the first page of students, sorted first by name and then by department, both in descending order.

Step 6: Pagination and Sorting Best Practices

- Default Values: Always set default values for pagination parameters (page, size, and sortBy) to ensure the API behaves predictably even when users don't specify these parameters.
- Response Structure: Spring Boot's Page object includes metadata (such as total pages and total elements), which helps clients understand the dataset's structure and navigate through pages.
- Performance Considerations: Use pagination for large datasets to reduce server load and improve response times. Avoid fetching all records at once.
- Sorting Flexibility: Allow users to sort by multiple fields and handle both ascending and descending orders for better user experience.

Conclusion

In this chapter, we explored how to implement pagination and sorting in a Spring Boot application with Spring Data JPA. We provided practical code examples, demonstrating how to efficiently paginate and sort data, using the Student API as a case study. By incorporating pagination and sorting, your application will be more scalable and user-friendly, particularly when handling large datasets.

In the next chapter, we will learn how to implement **file upload and download**. So stay tuned!

CHAPTER 12

FILE UPLOAD AND DOWNLOAD

In this chapter, we will explore how to implement file upload and download functionality in a Spring Boot application. Continuing with our Student Management API, we'll establish the capability to upload files such as student profile pictures or documents and create endpoints for downloading those files.

Why File Upload and Download?

In modern applications, it is common to require file management, whether it is documents, images, or other content. It doesn't matter if you are creating a student management application, content management system, or e-commerce site, adding file upload and download capabilities is all but almost always a must.

In this chapter, we will:
1. Make a pretty simple file storage class.
2. Write the necessary endpoints for the file upload and download.
3. Provide detailed code examples step by step

Step 1: Setting Up the Project

Before we commence with the code, let's make sure that we have no issues uploading the files in our Spring Boot project. If you are continuing on this from earlier posts, you already have the basic structure. Let's implement file-handling functionality.

Make sure you have these dependencies in your pom.xml:

```xml
<dependency>
    <groupId>org.springframework.boot</groupId>
    <artifactId>spring-boot-starter-web</artifactId>
</dependency>
<dependency>
    <groupId>org.springframework.boot</groupId>
    <artifactId>spring-boot-starter-data-jpa</artifactId>
</dependency>
<dependency>
    <groupId>com.h2database</groupId>
    <artifactId>h2</artifactId>
    <scope>runtime</scope>
</dependency>
```

Step 2: Configuring File Storage

For ease of implementation, we will keep the files on the local disk of the web application server. You can later change this to save files to cloud services like AWS S3 or Google Cloud storage.

Create a Directory for File Storage

First, create a directory to store files. In this example, we'll store files in a folder called uploads at the root of the project.

You can configure the directory path in your application.properties file:

```
file.upload-dir=uploads/
```

Step 3: Implementing File Upload

Let's create an endpoint to upload a file. We'll use Spring Boot's MultipartFile class to handle file uploads.

File Upload Service:

```java
@Service
public class FileStorageService {

    private final Path fileStorageLocation;

    // Inject the upload directory from application.properties
    public FileStorageService(@Value("${file.upload-dir}") String uploadDir) {
        this.fileStorageLocation = Paths.get(uploadDir)
                .toAbsolutePath().normalize();
        try {
            Files.createDirectories(this.fileStorageLocation);
        } catch (IOException e) {
            throw new RuntimeException("Could not create directory to store files", e);
        }
    }

    public String storeFile(MultipartFile file) {
        try {
            Path targetLocation = this.fileStorageLocation.resolve(file.getOriginalFilename());
            Files.copy(file.getInputStream(), targetLocation);
            return file.getOriginalFilename();
        } catch (IOException e) {
            throw new RuntimeException("Could not store file. Please try again!", e);
        }
    }
}
```

Explanation:

- The FileStorageService class is the one that implements the main logic of uploading and keeping the file in the uploads folder.
- The storeFile method accepts the uploaded file as a parameter, performs file saving operation on the specified target, and then returns the name of the file on success.

File Upload Controller:

```
import org.springframework.beans.factory.annotation.Autowired;
import org.springframework.http.ResponseEntity;
import org.springframework.web.bind.annotation.*;
import org.springframework.web.multipart.MultipartFile;

@RestController
@RequestMapping("/api/students/files")
public class FileController {

    @Autowired
    private FileStorageService fileStorageService;

    @PostMapping("/upload")
    public ResponseEntity<String> uploadFile(@RequestParam("file") MultipartFile file) {
        String fileName = fileStorageService.storeFile(file);
        return ResponseEntity.ok("File uploaded successfully: " + fileName);
    }
}
```

Explanation:

- The uploadFile method takes a file as an input parameter through the use of @RequestParam("file") annotation.
- The file is sent to FileStorageService, which stores it and returns a successful file name response to signify that the file has been uploaded.

Step 4: Implementing File Download

Next, we'll implement an endpoint to download the uploaded files.

File Download Service:

```
@Service
public class FileDownloadService {

    private final Path fileStorageLocation;

    public FileDownloadService() {
        this.fileStorageLocation = Paths.get("uploads")
                .toAbsolutePath().normalize();
    }
```

```java
public Resource loadFileAsResource(String fileName) {
    try {
        Path filePath = this.fileStorageLocation.resolve(fileName).normalize();
        Resource resource = new UrlResource(filePath.toUri());
        if (resource.exists()) {
            return resource;
        } else {
            throw new RuntimeException("File not found: " + fileName);
        }
    } catch (Exception e) {
        throw new RuntimeException("File not found: " + fileName, e);
    }
}
```

Explanation:

- The FileDownloadService loads the file as a Resource using Spring's UrlResource class, which is then used for download.
- If the file doesn't exist, it throws an exception.

File Download Controller:

```java
@RestController
@RequestMapping("/api/students/files")
public class FileController {

    @Autowired
    private FileDownloadService fileDownloadService;

    @GetMapping("/download/{fileName:.+}")
    public ResponseEntity<Resource> downloadFile(@PathVariable String fileName, HttpServletRequest request) {
        Resource resource = fileDownloadService.loadFileAsResource(fileName);

        String contentType;
        try {
            contentType = request.getServletContext().getMimeType(resource.getFile().getAbsolutePath());
        } catch (Exception e) {
            contentType = "application/octet-stream";
        }

        return ResponseEntity.ok()
                .contentType(MediaType.parseMediaType(contentType))
                .header(HttpHeaders.CONTENT_DISPOSITION, "attachment; filename=\"" + resource.getFilename() + "\"")
                .body(resource);
    }
}
```

Explanation:

- The downloadFile method accepts the fileName as a path variable and loads the file using FileDownloadService.
- It sets the appropriate MIME type for the file and includes a Content-Disposition header to force download.
- If the file type isn't determined, it defaults to application/octet-stream.

Step 5: Testing File Upload and Download

Now that we have both the upload and download functionality in place, let's test the API using **Postman** or **Curl**.

Uploading a File:

```
curl -F "file=@/path/to/your/file.jpg" http://localhost:8080/api/students/files/upload
```

Response:

```
{
    "message": "File uploaded successfully: file.jpg"
}
```

Downloading the File:

```
curl -O http://localhost:8080/api/students/files/download/file.jpg
```

This will download the file to your local machine.

Step 6: Handling Exceptions and Validations

In a production environment, you'll need to handle errors like file size limitations, unsupported file types, and non-existent files gracefully. Here are some best practices:

- **File Size Limitations**: You can set the maximum file size in application.properties:

```
spring.servlet.multipart.max-file-size=2MB
spring.servlet.multipart.max-request-size=2MB
```

- **Validation**: Add checks to ensure only certain file types (e.g., .jpg, .png, .pdf) are allowed for upload.

Conclusion

In this chapter, you learned how to implement **file upload and download** functionality in a Spring Boot application. We created endpoints for uploading and downloading files, explored how to store files locally, and discussed best practices for handling file-related operations.

In the next chapter, we will learn how to implement **thymeleaf with Spring Boot**. So stay tuned!

CHAPTER 13

SPRING BOOT WITH THYMELEAF

In this chapter, we'll learn how to integrate **Thymeleaf** with *Spring Boot* to create dynamic web pages. **Thymeleaf** is a Java-based template engine that works seamlessly with Spring Boot, making it an excellent choice for rendering web views. If you've been following along from the previous chapters, we've been developing a **Student Management API**. We will enhance the same project by adding web pages for managing students using Thymeleaf.

Why Thymeleaf?

Thymeleaf is quite often used as a rendering engine in Java applications, particularly in developing Spring Boot applications.

Some of the advantages of using Thymeleaf are:

- It works well with Spring Boot.
- It also provides natural templating that allows for rendering the templates as normal HTML pages without even the need for running a web server.
- It also supports list iteration, form data binding, and conditional content rendering which is very useful for web apps.

Step 1: Setting Up Thymeleaf in Spring Boot

To get started, you need to add the **Thymeleaf** dependency to your pom.xml file:

pom.xml

```xml
<dependency>
    <groupId>org.springframework.boot</groupId>
    <artifactId>spring-boot-starter-thymeleaf</artifactId>
</dependency>
<dependency>
    <groupId>org.springframework.boot</groupId>
    <artifactId>spring-boot-starter-web</artifactId>
</dependency>
<dependency>
    <groupId>org.springframework.boot</groupId>
    <artifactId>spring-boot-starter-data-jpa</artifactId>
</dependency>
<dependency>
    <groupId>com.h2database</groupId>
    <artifactId>h2</artifactId>
    <scope>runtime</scope>
</dependency>
```

These dependencies ensure that you have **Thymeleaf**, **Spring MVC**, and **JPA** set up, as well as an in-memory **H2** database.

Step 2: Create the Student Entity

We will continue using the Student entity from previous tutorials. Here's a quick recap of what the Student class looks like:

Student.java

```java
@Entity
public class Student {

    @Id
    @GeneratedValue(strategy = GenerationType.IDENTITY)
    private Long id;
    private String name;
    private String email;
    private String course;

    // Constructors, getters, and setters
    public Student() {
    }

    public Student(String name, String email, String course) {
        this.name = name;
        this.email = email;
        this.course = course;
    }

    // Getters and setters
}
```

Step 3: Create a Student Repository

To access the database, we'll create a simple JPA repository for the Student entity.

StudentRepository.java

```java
import org.springframework.data.jpa.repository.JpaRepository;
import org.springframework.stereotype.Repository;

@Repository
public interface StudentRepository extends JpaRepository<Student, Long> {
}
```

Step 4: Create the Controller for Handling Requests

Now, let's create a Spring MVC controller to handle the HTTP requests and return Thymeleaf views.

StudentController.java

```java
@Controller
@RequestMapping("/students")
public class StudentController {

    @Autowired
    private StudentRepository studentRepository;

    @GetMapping
    public String viewStudents(Model model) {
        List<Student> students = studentRepository.findAll();
        model.addAttribute("students", students);
        return "students";
    }

    @GetMapping("/new")
    public String createStudentForm(Model model) {
        model.addAttribute("student", new Student());
        return "create_student";
    }

    @PostMapping
    public String saveStudent(@ModelAttribute("student") Student student) {
        studentRepository.save(student);
        return "redirect:/students";
    }

    @GetMapping("/edit/{id}")
    public String editStudentForm(@PathVariable Long id, Model model) {
        Student student = studentRepository.findById(id).orElseThrow(() -> new
IllegalArgumentException("Invalid student Id:" + id));
        model.addAttribute("student", student);
        return "edit_student";
    }

    @PostMapping("/update/{id}")
    public String updateStudent(@PathVariable Long id, @ModelAttribute("student") Student student) {
        studentRepository.save(student);
        return "redirect:/students";
    }

    @GetMapping("/delete/{id}")
    public String deleteStudent(@PathVariable Long id) {
        studentRepository.deleteById(id);
        return "redirect:/students";
    }
}
```

Explanation:

- @GetMapping("/students"): Handles the request to display all students.
- @GetMapping("/students/new"): Displays the form to create a new student.
- @PostMapping("/students"): Handles the form submission to save a new student.

- @GetMapping("/edit/{id}"): Fetches the student by ID and returns the edit form.
- @PostMapping("/update/{id}"): Updates the student in the database.
- @GetMapping("/delete/{id}"): Deletes the student by ID.

Step 5: Create Thymeleaf Templates

Now, let's create the Thymeleaf templates to display and manage student data.

students.html (View all students)

```html
<!DOCTYPE html>
<html xmlns:th="http://www.thymeleaf.org">
<head>
    <title>Students</title>
</head>
<body>
<h1>Student List</h1>
<a href="/students/new">Add New Student</a>
<table border="1">
    <thead>
        <tr>
            <th>ID</th>
            <th>Name</th>
            <th>Email</th>
            <th>Course</th>
            <th>Actions</th>
        </tr>
    </thead>
    <tbody>
        <tr th:each="student : ${students}">
            <td th:text="${student.id}"></td>
            <td th:text="${student.name}"></td>
            <td th:text="${student.email}"></td>
            <td th:text="${student.course}"></td>
            <td>
                <a th:href="@{/students/edit/{id}(id=${student.id})}">Edit</a> |
                <a th:href="@{/students/delete/{id}(id=${student.id})}">Delete</a>
            </td>
        </tr>
    </tbody>
</table>
</body>
</html>
```

students.html (View all students)

```html
<!DOCTYPE html>
<html xmlns:th="http://www.thymeleaf.org">
<head>
    <title>Add Student</title>
</head>
<body>
<h1>Add New Student</h1>
<form th:action="@{/students}" th:object="${student}" method="post">
    <label for="name">Name:</label>
    <input type="text" id="name" th:field="*{name}" /><br>

    <label for="email">Email:</label>
    <input type="email" id="email" th:field="*{email}" /><br>

    <label for="course">Course:</label>
    <input type="text" id="course" th:field="*{course}" /><br>

    <button type="submit">Save</button>
</form>
</body>
</html>
```

edit_student.html (Form to edit an existing student)

```html
<!DOCTYPE html>
<html xmlns:th="http://www.thymeleaf.org">
<head>
    <title>Edit Student</title>
</head>
<body>
<h1>Edit Student</h1>
<form th:action="@{/students/update/{id}(id=${student.id})}" th:object="${student}" method="post">
    <label for="name">Name:</label>
    <input type="text" id="name" th:field="*{name}" /><br>

    <label for="email">Email:</label>
    <input type="email" id="email" th:field="*{email}" /><br>

    <label for="course">Course:</label>
    <input type="text" id="course" th:field="*{course}" /><br>

    <button type="submit">Update</button>
</form>
</body>
</html>
```

118

Step 6: Testing the Application

1. Run the Spring Boot application.
2. Visit http://localhost:8080/students to view the list of students.
3. Add, edit, or delete students using the web forms.

Conclusion

This chapter aimed to **integrate Spring Boot and Thymeleaf** so as to create dynamic webpages for our Student Management Application. We explored the creation of the needed views, the processing of user inputs, and the storage of this information in a database. The templating capabilities offered by Thymeleaf render it easy to create attractive web interfaces for Spring Boot applications.

In the next chapter, we will learn how to consume **external APIs in Spring Boot**. So stay tuned!

CHAPTER 14

CONSUMING EXTERNAL APIS

In this chapter, we'll shift gears and delve into how to consume external APIs using Spring Boot. This skill is crucial for building microservices, integrating third-party services, or retrieving external data for your application

What Does "Consuming an API" Mean?

In web development, consuming an API refers to your application making a request to another service (typically a third-party API) and utilizing the data that the service returns. For instance, your Student Management API might need to gather external information such as weather updates, currency exchange rates, or even student data from other platforms. In this tutorial, we'll make HTTP requests to an external API and showcase that data in our application.

Step 1: Set Up RestTemplate or WebClient

Spring Boot provides two common ways to consume external REST APIs:
- RestTemplate (older and more commonly used)
- WebClient (the newer and more modern option in Spring WebFlux)

We'll focus on both approaches, starting with RestTemplate. You can use either based on your preference.

Add Dependencies

In the pom.xml, ensure you have the required dependencies:

```
<dependency>
    <groupId>org.springframework.boot</groupId>
    <artifactId>spring-boot-starter-web</artifactId>
</dependency>
```

This adds the necessary Spring Web module to make HTTP requests.

Step 2: Using RestTemplate to Consume an API

First, we'll utilize the RestTemplate class from Spring's web module to access an external API. For instance, if you want to retrieve information about students from a remote service, here's how you can do it.

RestTemplate Bean Configuration

```java
import org.springframework.context.annotation.Bean;
import org.springframework.context.annotation.Configuration;
import org.springframework.web.client.RestTemplate;

@Configuration
public class RestTemplateConfig {

    @Bean
    public RestTemplate restTemplate() {
        return new RestTemplate();
    }
}
```

This configuration defines a RestTemplate bean that we can inject into other components.

Step 3: Consuming an External API with RestTemplate

Let's develop a service that utilizes a mock student API and incorporates the data into our application. For demonstration purposes, we'll use an API endpoint such as <u>First, we'll utilize the RestTemplate class from Spring's web module to access an external API. For instance, if you want to retrieve information about students from a remote service, here's how you can do it.</u>

StudentService.java

```java
import org.springframework.beans.factory.annotation.Autowired;
import org.springframework.stereotype.Service;
import org.springframework.web.client.RestTemplate;
import java.util.Arrays;
import java.util.List;

@Service
public class StudentService {

    @Autowired
    private RestTemplate restTemplate;

    private final String EXTERNAL_API_URL = "https://jsonplaceholder.typicode.com/users";

    public List<Object> getExternalStudents() {
        Object[] students = restTemplate.getForObject(EXTERNAL_API_URL, Object[].class);
        return Arrays.asList(students);
    }
}
```

Explanation:

- We define the external API: <u>https://jsonplaceholder.typicode.com/users.</u>
- restTemplate.getForObject() is used to make a **GET** request to the external API.
- The result is an array of objects, which we convert into a list and return.

Step 4: Displaying External API Data in a Controller

Now let's create a controller that will display the external data returned by the StudentService in our view.

StudentController.java

```java
import org.springframework.beans.factory.annotation.Autowired;
import org.springframework.stereotype.Controller;
import org.springframework.ui.Model;
import org.springframework.web.bind.annotation.GetMapping;

@Controller
public class StudentController {

    @Autowired
    private StudentService studentService;

    @GetMapping("/external-students")
    public String viewExternalStudents(Model model) {
        model.addAttribute("students", studentService.getExternalStudents());
        return "external_students";
    }

}
```

In this controller, the '/external-students' endpoint calls the getExternalStudents() method from the service to fetch the external data and pass it to the view.

Step 5: Creating a Thymeleaf View

Next, we'll create a Thymeleaf template to display the external students we fetched from the API.

external_students.html

```
<!DOCTYPE html>
<html xmlns:th="http://www.thymeleaf.org">
<head>
    <title>External Students</title>
</head>
<body>
<h1>External Student List</h1>
<table border="1">
    <thead>
        <tr>
            <th>ID</th>
            <th>Name</th>
            <th>Username</th>
            <th>Email</th>
        </tr>
    </thead>
    <tbody>
        <tr th:each="student : ${students}">
            <td th:text="${student['id']}"></td>
            <td th:text="${student['name']}"></td>
            <td th:text="${student['username']}"></td>
            <td th:text="${student['email']}"></td>
        </tr>
    </tbody>
</table>
</body>
</html>
```

Explanation:

- In this template, we loop through the list of students using th:each.
- Since we're dealing with JSON data returned by the external API, we access the fields dynamically (e.g., student['id'], student['name']).

Step 6: Running the Application

1. Start the Spring Boot application.
2. Visit http://localhost:8080/external-students to see the list of students fetched from the external API.

Step 7: Using WebClient for Reactive API Consumption

Now, let's see how to use WebClient, the modern alternative to RestTemplate, which is non-blocking and better suited for reactive programming.

WebClient Bean Configuration

```java
import org.springframework.context.annotation.Bean;
import org.springframework.context.annotation.Configuration;
import org.springframework.web.reactive.function.client.WebClient;

@Configuration
public class WebClientConfig {

    @Bean
    public WebClient.Builder webClientBuilder() {
        return WebClient.builder();
    }
}
```

Consuming an External API with WebClient

Here's how you would fetch the same external data using WebClient:

```java
import org.springframework.beans.factory.annotation.Autowired;
import org.springframework.stereotype.Service;
import org.springframework.web.reactive.function.client.WebClient;
import reactor.core.publisher.Mono;
import java.util.List;

@Service
public class StudentService {

    @Autowired
    private WebClient.Builder webClientBuilder;

    private final String EXTERNAL_API_URL = "https://jsonplaceholder.typicode.com/users";

    public Mono<List<Object>> getExternalStudents() {
        return webClientBuilder.build()
                .get()
                .uri(EXTERNAL_API_URL)
                .retrieve()
                .bodyToMono(List.class);
    }
}
```

Explanation:

- WebClient is used here to perform a non-blocking request.
- The result is a Mono of a list of students, which represents a reactive type that emits a single value asynchronously.

Conclusion

In this chapter, we looked at how to interact with external APIs in Spring Boot, utilizing both RestTemplate and WebClient. We showed how to retrieve student data from a mock external API and present it in a web view with Thymeleaf. Depending on your application's requirements, you can opt for either method — RestTemplate for straightforward scenarios and WebClient for reactive applications.

In the upcoming chapter, we will delve into **Spring Boot Actuator Introduction**. Stay tuned!

CHAPTER 15

INTRODUCTION TO SPRING BOOT ACTUATOR

We will consider one of the most convenient tools of the Spring framework in this article — Spring Boot Actuator. We will define what the actuator is, learn how to implement it in a Spring Boot application, and explain how it can assist you in observing the health, metrics, and other aspects of your application

What is Spring Boot Actuator?

The **Spring Boot actuator** includes several features necessary for monitoring and managing the application. It is helpful in monitoring and operations of the app by generating several endpoints that contain metrics, health status, environment, etc.

Some key features of Spring Boot Actuator include:
- Monitoring the health of your application.
- Tracking important metrics (e.g., **memory usage**, **CPU load**).
- Viewing configuration properties and beans.
- Interacting with your application during runtime using HTTP endpoints.

Let's see how we can set up and implement Spring Boot Actuator in our Student Management API.

Step 1: Configuring Spring Boot Actuator's Interface

Add the Actuator Dependency

At this point, you need to introduce the Spring Boot Actuator dependency to the pom.xml file.

```xml
<dependency>
  <groupId>org.springframework.boot</groupId>
  <artifactId>spring-boot-starter-actuator</artifactId>
</dependency>
```

The above-added source will also bring all the dependencies that are needed to run the Spring Boot Actuator in your project.

Step 2: Configuring Actuator in application.properties

Under normal circumstances, only some Actuator endpoints are enabled by default. To allow for additional options, you should edit your application.properties file.

```
# Enable all actuator endpoints
management.endpoints.web.exposure.include=*
```

The above configuration exposes all the Actuator endpoints along with the endpoints including /health, /metrics, /info etc. Extremities should be exercised when exposing such in production levels to avoid compromising security.

Step 3: Exploring Actuator Endpoints

Since we have configured the Actuator, let's see some of the noteworthy endpoints that are used quite frequently:

- **/actuator/health**: Provides information regarding the health of the application.
- **/actuator/metrics**: Displays information on metrics such as used memory and CPU utilization, requests made, etc.
- **/actuator/info**: Gives information about the application, it can be modified if necessary.

Now to validate these endpoints, run your Spring Boot application and browse to http://localhost:8080/actuator/health using Postman or web browser.

Step 4: Implementing Spring Boot Actuator in the Student API

Let's continue with our Student Management API example and integrate Actuator to monitor its health and metrics.

Health Endpoint Example

The **/actuator/health** endpoint shows the status of the application. By default, it returns either UP (healthy) or DOWN (unhealthy). You can customize this endpoint to include additional health checks, such as checking the database connection or external services.

Custom Health Indicator

Let's create a custom health indicator that checks if our **Student API** is connected to the database.

```java
import org.springframework.boot.actuate.health.Health;
import org.springframework.boot.actuate.health.HealthIndicator;
import org.springframework.stereotype.Component;

@Component
public class StudentServiceHealthIndicator implements HealthIndicator {
```

```java
@Override
public Health health() {
    // Simulate a database check or API connection
    boolean databaseUp = checkDatabaseConnection();

    if (databaseUp) {
        return Health.up().withDetail("Database", "Running").build();
    } else {
        return Health.down().withDetail("Database", "Not reachable").build();
    }
}

private boolean checkDatabaseConnection() {
    // Logic to check database connection
    return true; // Replace with actual database check
}
}
```

In this example:

- The StudentServiceHealthIndicator class checks the status of the database connection.
- If the database is reachable, the health status is marked as UP. Otherwise, it returns DOWN.

When you visit /actuator/health, you'll now see custom information about the database connection.

Step 5: Monitoring Metrics

One of the most powerful features of Actuator is the capability of obtaining metrics of your application. The /actuator/metrics endpoint outputs information on various system metrics like memory, CPU, request, and many others.

Our goal here will be to track some of the basic metrics, for example, the count of HTTP requests on our Student API.

Track API Metrics

By default, Spring Boot Actuator tracks metrics for every HTTP request your application receives. You can access these metrics via the /actuator/metrics/http.server.requests endpoint.

In relation to the above, in order to check the number of requests sent to a particular endpoint, for example, /students, one can utilize this endpoint with the following URL:

```
http://localhost:8080/actuator/metrics/http.server.requests
?tag=uri:/students
```

It will return the number of requests made to the endpoint and other related information such as response time and other metrics around the /students endpoint.

Step 6: Display Application Info

The **/actuator/info** endpoint can be customized to show additional details about your application. You can configure it in your application.properties file.

```
info.app.name=Student Management API
info.app.description=API to manage students
info.app.version=1.0.0
info.app.name=Student Management API
```

When you visit /actuator/info, you'll see this information displayed:

```json
{
  "app": {
    "name": "Student Management API",
    "description": "API to manage students",
    "version": "1.0.0"
  }
}
```

Step 7: Securing Actuator Endpoints

In production environments, it's important to secure your Actuator endpoints to prevent unauthorized access. Spring Boot makes this easy by integrating with **Spring Security**.

Let's add basic authentication to secure the Actuator endpoints.

Add Security Dependency

First, add the Spring Security dependency to your pom.xml:

```xml
<dependency>
    <groupId>org.springframework.boot</groupId>
    <artifactId>spring-boot-starter-security</artifactId>
</dependency>
```

Configure Security for Actuator

In your application.properties, you can configure basic authentication for the Actuator endpoints:

```
# Enable basic security for actuator
management.endpoints.web.exposure.include=*
management.endpoint.health.show-details=always
management.endpoints.web.exposure.exclude=env,beans,threaddump
spring.security.user.name=admin
spring.security.user.password=admin123
```

Now, when you try to access the Actuator endpoints, you'll be prompted to enter the credentials (**admin/admin123**).

Step 8: Monitoring the Application with Actuator in Production

To monitor your Spring Boot application in production, you can integrate Actuator with monitoring tools like **Prometheus** and **Grafana**. These tools help visualize the metrics exposed by the Actuator in real-time.

For example, Actuator provides a **Prometheus-compatible metrics endpoint** (/actuator/prometheus) that can be scraped by Prometheus, which can then be visualized in Grafana.

Conclusion

In this chapter, we have discussed fundamental concepts associated with Spring Boot Actuator. We have demonstrated the use of the Actuator to monitor the health and performance of the Student Management API. We configured custom health endpoints, measured the API usage, and implemented Spring Security on the Actuator endpoints for protection. This feature comes to great use when combined with monitoring tools as it will be possible to monitor the status of the application deployed in a production environment.

In next chapter, we will see how to use Spring Boot profiles and set up environment configurations.

CHAPTER 16

SPRING BOOT PROFILES AND ENVIRONMENT CONFIGURATION

In this chapter, we will learn about the most important concept to create a production-ready application: Spring Boot Profiles and Environment Configuration.

In this article, We will learn :

1. What are Spring Boot profiles
2. How to create and configure profiles
3. How to implement the profiles in Spring Boot
4. Setting up profiles for traditional Development, Test, and Production environments
5. Key things to keep in mind when using profiles

We'll continue using the **Student Management API** example to illustrate these concepts

What are Spring Boot Profiles?

In Spring Boot, profiles allow you to define different configurations that are about different environments such as development, testing, etc. Each environment may have different and specific configurations for:

- **Database connections.**
- **Logging levels.**
- **Details of upstream/downstream systems.**

Spring Boot makes it easy to manage multiple environments through profiles, allowing you to run your application in different environments without manually changing your configuration files.

Why Use Profiles?

- **Environment-specific configurations**: Each environment (dev, test, prod) has unique needs.
- **Maintainability**: Keep your configuration clean and separate.
- **Flexibility**: Quickly switch between environments during development and deployment.

Step 1: Creating a Spring Boot Profile

To create a Spring Boot profile, all you need to do is create different configuration files for each profile and use them based on the active environment.

Naming Convention for Profiles

Spring Boot supports the following naming convention for profile-based configuration files:

```
application-{profile}.properties
```

For example:

- application-dev.properties — Configuration for the development environment.
- application-test.properties — Configuration for the testing environment.
- application-prod.properties — Configuration for the production environment.

Step 2: Setting Up Profiles in the Student API Example

Let's implement profiles in our **Student Management API** to handle different configurations for development, testing, and production.

Default Configuration (application.properties)

The default configuration file, application.properties, will be used when no profile is active. Here, we'll define the basic properties that apply to all environments.

```
# Default configuration
server.port=8080
spring.datasource.url=jdbc:h2:mem:testdb
spring.datasource.driverClassName=org.h2.Driver
spring.datasource.username=sa
spring.datasource.password=password
```

This configuration uses an in-memory **H2 database**, which is useful for testing and development purposes.

Step 3: Creating Environment-Specific Profiles

Now, let's create profiles for **development**, **testing**, and **production** environments.

Default Configuration (application.properties)

In the development profile, you might want to enable debugging, use a local database, and configure relaxed security.

```
# Dev environment
server.port=8081
spring.datasource.url=jdbc:mysql://localhost:3306/student_dev
spring.datasource.username=dev_user
spring.datasource.password=dev_password
spring.jpa.hibernate.ddl-auto=update
logging.level.org.springframework=DEBUG
```

This configuration:

- Runs the application on port **8081**.
- Connects to a local MySQL database for development purposes.
- Sets Hibernate to update the schema automatically.
- Enables detailed logging for debugging.

Testing Profile (application-test.properties)

For testing, we usually use a lightweight database (like H2) and ensure that all settings are isolated from production or development environments.

```
# Test environment
server.port=8082
spring.datasource.url=jdbc:h2:mem:testdb
spring.datasource.driverClassName=org.h2.Driver
spring.datasource.username=sa
spring.datasource.password=password
spring.jpa.hibernate.ddl-auto=create-drop
```

This configuration:
- Runs the application on port 8082.
- Uses an in-memory H2 database for testing.
- Automatically creates and drops the schema after each test run.

Production Profile (application-prod.properties)

In the production profile, it's critical to set up connections to production databases, optimize performance, and ensure logging is appropriately configured.

```
# Prod environment
server.port=80
spring.datasource.url=jdbc:mysql://prod-db-server:3306/student_prod
spring.datasource.username=prod_user
spring.datasource.password=prod_password
spring.jpa.hibernate.ddl-auto=none
logging.level.org.springframework=ERROR
```

This configuration:
- Runs the application on port 80 (the default HTTP port).
- Connects to a production MySQL database.
- Disables Hibernate schema auto-update for better control over the database schema.
- Limits logging to only critical errors.

Step 4: Activating Profiles

To activate a profile, you can specify the **active profile** in several ways:

1. Using application.properties

In the application.properties file, you can set the active profile like this:

```
spring.profiles.active=dev
```

This will activate the dev profile when the application starts.

2. Using Command-Line Arguments

You can also activate a profile via the command line when running your Spring Boot application:

```
mvn spring-boot:run -Dspring-boot.run.profiles=prod
```

This command runs the application with the **prod** profile.

3. Using Environment Variables

You can set the active profile as an environment variable, which is useful in cloud environments:

```
export SPRING_PROFILES_ACTIVE=prod
```

Step 5: Profile-Specific Beans

Sometimes, you need to create beans that are only active for certain profiles. You can use the @Profile annotation to achieve this.

Example: Creating Beans for Different Profiles

In the **Student Management API**, you might want to have different services for different environments. Let's create a service that's only active in the development environment.

```java
@Service
@Profile("dev")
public class DevStudentService implements StudentService {
    @Override
    public String getStudentDetails() {
        return "Development Student Service: Fetching data from Dev Database";
    }
}
```

This DevStudentService will only be active when the dev profile is enabled.

Step 6: Key Considerations for Using Profiles

When working with Spring Boot profiles, there are a few important things to keep in mind:

1. Avoid Hardcoding Secrets

Don't hardcode sensitive information (e.g., database credentials, API keys) in your profile files. Use external configuration management tools or environment variables to manage sensitive data securely.

2. Test Each Profile

Make sure to test your application in each environment profile to ensure that the configurations work as expected. This is especially important for the production environment, where configuration errors can have critical impacts.

3. Leverage Environment Variables

Use environment variables to make your configuration flexible and avoid duplication in your profile files. For example, you can pass the database URL or credentials as environment variables instead of hardcoding them in your properties files.

Conclusion

In this chapter, we explored how to use **Spring Boot profiles** to manage different configurations for development, testing, and production environments. We learned how to create and configure profiles, activate them using various methods, and manage profile-specific beans in our **Student Management API** example.

By leveraging profiles, you can build flexible, environment-specific applications that are easy to maintain and scale.

CHAPTER 17

LOGGING

In this chapter, we'll cover an essential aspect of any application: Logging. Logging provides insights into your application's behavior, helps in debugging, and enables monitoring in production environments.

We'll continue with the Student Management API as our reference project.

Overview of Logging in Spring Boot

By default, Spring Boot uses Logback for logging. Logback is a reliable and fast logging framework that is fully integrated with Spring Boot. It also supports SLF4J, a widely-used logging API, providing flexibility to plug in other logging frameworks.

Here's a high-level breakdown of the logging system:

- **SLF4J** is a simple logging façade, allowing you to log in with a common API.
- **Logback** is the default logging implementation in Spring Boot.

Spring Boot logs at different levels: ERROR, WARN, INFO, DEBUG, and TRACE. Each level controls the amount of detail you see in the logs.

Configuring Logging in Spring Boot

Spring Boot provides an out-of-the-box logging configuration, but it also allows you to customize it through properties files or XML configuration files.

Default Logging Configuration

In a new Spring Boot project, logging is already enabled with sensible defaults. The default logger is configured to output to the console.

To see this, let's add a simple log statement in our **Student Management API**.

Example: Default Logging

```java
@RestController
@RequestMapping("/students")
public class StudentController {

    private static final Logger logger = LoggerFactory.getLogger(StudentController.class);

    @GetMapping("/{id}")
    public ResponseEntity<Student> getStudentById(@PathVariable Long id) {
        logger.info("Fetching student with ID: {}", id); // Logging a message
        // Business logic to fetch student by ID
        return ResponseEntity.ok(new Student(id, "John Doe", "john.doe@example.com"));
    }
}
```

In this example, the log level is set to INFO. When you hit the /students/{id} endpoint, you'll see the following log output in the console:

INFO 12345 --- [nio-8080-exec-1] c.example.demo.StudentController : Fetching student with ID: 1

Customizing Logging in Spring Boot

You can customize the logging levels and output locations using the application.properties or application.yml file.

Changing Logging Levels

To change the log level, you can define properties in your application.properties file.

```
# Set root logging level to WARN (default is INFO)
logging.level.root=WARN

# Enable DEBUG logging for the StudentController class
logging.level.com.example.demo.StudentController=DEBUG
```

With this setup, the application will log only warnings and errors at the root level, but it will log debug messages from the StudentController class.

Writing Logs to a File

You can also configure Spring Boot to write logs to a file.

```
# Enable logging to a file
logging.file.name=student-api.log

# Set maximum file size
logging.file.max-size=10MB
```

This configuration will write logs to the student-api.log file in the root directory, with a maximum size of 10MB.

Setting Up Logback in Spring Boot

Logback is the default logging framework in Spring Boot, and it's highly customizable. You can configure Logback using an XML file (logback-spring.xml) for more advanced setups.

Basic Logback Configuration

Create a logback-spring.xml file in the src/main/resources directory.

```xml
<configuration>

    <!-- Console Appender -->
    <appender name="CONSOLE" class="ch.qos.logback.core.ConsoleAppender">
        <encoder>
            <pattern>%d{yyyy-MM-dd HH:mm:ss} [%thread] %-5level %logger{36} - %msg%n</pattern>
        </encoder>
    </appender>

    <!-- File Appender -->
    <appender name="FILE" class="ch.qos.logback.core.FileAppender">
        <file>logs/student-api.log</file>
        <encoder>
            <pattern>%d{yyyy-MM-dd HH:mm:ss} [%thread] %-5level %logger{36} - %msg%n</pattern>
        </encoder>
    </appender>

    <!-- Root Logger -->
    <root level="INFO">
        <appender-ref ref="CONSOLE" />
        <appender-ref ref="FILE" />
    </root>

    <!-- Logger for specific class -->
    <logger name="com.example.demo.StudentController" level="DEBUG" />

</configuration>
```

In this configuration:

- Logs are sent both to the console and a file (logs/student-api.log).
- We've set the log level to INFO for all classes, but DEBUG for StudentController.

Rolling Files Configuration

You can also configure **rolling files** to avoid your log file becoming too large.

```xml
<appender name="ROLLING" class="ch.qos.logback.core.rolling.RollingFileAppender">
    <file>logs/student-api.log</file>
    <rollingPolicy class="ch.qos.logback.core.rolling.TimeBasedRollingPolicy">
        <!-- Roll logs every day -->
        <fileNamePattern>logs/student-api-%d{yyyy-MM-dd}.log</fileNamePattern>
        <maxHistory>30</maxHistory> <!-- Keep 30 days of logs -->
    </rollingPolicy>
    <encoder>
        <pattern>%d{yyyy-MM-dd HH:mm:ss} [%thread] %-5level %logger{36} - %msg%n</pattern>
    </encoder>
</appender>
```

In this configuration, a new log file will be created each day, and Spring Boot will keep logs for the last 30 days.

Using SLF4J with Spring Boot

SLF4J (Simple Logging Facade for Java) is a popular logging API, and Spring Boot uses it as an abstraction layer over the logging implementation (e.g., Logback).

SLF4J in Action

Here's how you can use SLF4J in the Student Management API.

```java
import org.slf4j.Logger;
import org.slf4j.LoggerFactory;
import org.springframework.web.bind.annotation.*;

@RestController
@RequestMapping("/students")
public class StudentController {

    private static final Logger logger = LoggerFactory.getLogger(StudentController.class);

    @PostMapping
    public ResponseEntity<Student> addStudent(@RequestBody Student student) {
        logger.info("Adding a new student: {}", student.getName());
        // Business logic to add student
        return ResponseEntity.ok(student);
    }

    @GetMapping("/{id}")
    public ResponseEntity<Student> getStudentById(@PathVariable Long id) {
        logger.debug("Fetching student with ID: {}", id);
        // Business logic to fetch student
        return ResponseEntity.ok(new Student(id, "John Doe", "john.doe@example.com"));
    }
}
```

In this example, we're using **SLF4J** to log messages in both the addStudent and getStudentById methods.

Key Considerations for Logging

When setting up logging in Spring Boot, there are a few things to keep in mind:

1. Log Levels

- Use different log levels (ERROR, WARN, INFO, DEBUG, TRACE) appropriately.
- Avoid logging sensitive information such as passwords or personal data.

2. Log Rotation

- Make sure to configure log rotation to avoid large log files.
- Log files should be manageable and easy to search through when debugging.

3. Use Asynchronous Logging (For High Traffic Apps)

- In high-traffic applications, consider using asynchronous logging to avoid blocking the main thread while writing logs.

Conclusion

In this chapter, we've learned how to configure and customize logging in Spring Boot using **Logback** and **SLF4J**. We implemented logging in our **Student Management API**, configured custom logging levels, set up file logging, and explored Logback's rolling file strategy.

Logging is a critical part of monitoring and maintaining your application in production. By following the tips and practices shared in this chapter, you can ensure that your logs provide valuable insights into the health and behavior of your application.

CHAPTER 18

UNIT TESTING

In this chapter, we will see how to perform unit tests and integration tests in Spring Boot using JUnit and Mockito, also we will examine the testing of REST APIs using MockMvc. Such actions are inherent while creating any substantial application. With Spring Boot, it is easier because it comes with full-fledged support for testing.

Overview of Testing in Spring Boot

Spring Boot has testing support out of the box and is compatible with both Junit5 and Mockito testing frameworks. Testing with Spring Boot can be broadly classified in two ways:

1. **Unit Testing**: This refers to the tests that are done on every component that is created in isolation. This includes, but is not limited to services and, controllers.
2. **Integration Testing**: Tests on the interface between the various components. For example different REST API endpoints.

In this chapter, we'll focus on:
- Writing unit tests with **JUnit 5** and **Mockito**.
- Testing REST APIs using **MockMvc**.

Step 1: Setting Up Dependencies

Before diving into the examples, ensure you have the required dependencies in your pom.xml.

```xml
<dependencies>
    <!-- Spring Boot Starter Test -->
    <dependency>
        <groupId>org.springframework.boot</groupId>
        <artifactId>spring-boot-starter-test</artifactId>
        <scope>test</scope>
    </dependency>

    <!-- Mockito Core -->
    <dependency>
        <groupId>org.mockito</groupId>
        <artifactId>mockito-core</artifactId>
        <scope>test</scope>
    </dependency>
</dependencies>
```

Spring Boot Starter Test includes **JUnit**, **Mockito**, and **Spring's** testing libraries, providing a solid foundation for testing.

Step 2: Writing Unit Tests with JUnit and Mockito

In this portion, we will perform unit testing for the service layer of our Student Management API. We will be utilizing Mockito to create the mocks and JUnit for the test.

StudentService Class

Here's a simplified class for StudentService, which is meant to contain and manage student-related business logic:

```java
@Service
public class StudentService {

    @Autowired
    private StudentRepository studentRepository;
```

```
public Student getStudentById(Long id) {
    return studentRepository.findById(id)
            .orElseThrow(() -> new RuntimeException("Student not found"));
}

public Student addStudent(Student student) {
    return studentRepository.save(student);
}
}
```

Writing Unit Tests

Now, let's write unit tests for the StudentService class. We'll use **Mockito** to mock the StudentRepository.

```java
@SpringBootTest
class StudentServiceTest {

    @Mock
    private StudentRepository studentRepository;

    @InjectMocks
    private StudentService studentService;

    @Test
    void testGetStudentById_Success() {
        // Arrange
        Long studentId = 1L;
        Student student = new Student(studentId, "John Doe", "john.doe@example.com");
        Mockito.when(studentRepository.findById(studentId)).thenReturn(Optional.of(student));

        // Act
        Student result = studentService.getStudentById(studentId);

        // Assert
        assertEquals("John Doe", result.getName());
        assertEquals("john.doe@example.com", result.getEmail());
    }

    @Test
    void testGetStudentById_ThrowsException() {
        // Arrange
        Long studentId = 1L;
        Mockito.when(studentRepository.findById(studentId)).thenReturn(Optional.empty());

        // Act & Assert
        assertThrows(RuntimeException.class, () -> studentService.getStudentById(studentId));
    }

    @Test
    void testAddStudent() {
        // Arrange
        Student student = new Student(null, "Jane Doe", "jane.doe@example.com");
        Mockito.when(studentRepository.save(student)).thenReturn(new Student(1L, "Jane Doe",
"jane.doe@example.com"));

        // Act
        Student result = studentService.addStudent(student);

        // Assert
        assertNotNull(result.getId());
        assertEquals("Jane Doe", result.getName());
    }
}
```

Explanation:

- **@Mock**: We use Mockito's @Mock annotation to create a mock instance of StudentRepository.
- **@InjectMocks**: Inject the mock dependencies into the StudentService class.
- **Mockito.when**: Mock the behavior of studentRepository.findById() and studentRepository.save() methods.
- **assertThrows**: Verifies that an exception is thrown when the student is not found.

Step 3: Testing REST APIs with MockMvc

Testing REST APIs is crucial to ensure that your endpoints behave as expected. Spring Boot provides **MockMvc**, a powerful testing tool for simulating HTTP requests and verifying the responses.

Let's write tests for the StudentController class.

StudentController Class

```java
@RestController
@RequestMapping("/students")
public class StudentController {

    @Autowired
    private StudentService studentService;

    @GetMapping("/{id}")
    public ResponseEntity<Student> getStudentById(@PathVariable Long id) {
        Student student = studentService.getStudentById(id);
        return ResponseEntity.ok(student);
    }

    @PostMapping
    public ResponseEntity<Student> addStudent(@RequestBody Student student) {
        Student createdStudent = studentService.addStudent(student);
        return ResponseEntity.status(HttpStatus.CREATED).body(createdStudent);
    }
}
```

Writing REST API Tests

Let's write tests for the getStudentById and addStudent endpoints using **MockMvc**.

```java
@SpringBootTest
@AutoConfigureMockMvc
class StudentControllerTest {

    @Autowired
    private MockMvc mockMvc;

    @MockBean
    private StudentService studentService;

    @Test
    void testGetStudentById_Success() throws Exception {
        // Arrange
        Long studentId = 1L;
        Student student = new Student(studentId, "John Doe", "john.doe@example.com");
        Mockito.when(studentService.getStudentById(studentId)).thenReturn(student);

        // Act & Assert
        mockMvc.perform(get("/students/{id}", studentId))
                .andExpect(status().isOk())
                .andExpect(jsonPath("$.name").value("John Doe"))
                .andExpect(jsonPath("$.email").value("john.doe@example.com"));
    }

    @Test
    void testAddStudent_Success() throws Exception {
        // Arrange
        Student student = new Student(null, "Jane Doe", "jane.doe@example.com");
        Mockito.when(studentService.addStudent(Mockito.any(Student.class)))
                .thenReturn(new Student(1L, "Jane Doe", "jane.doe@example.com"));

        // Act & Assert
        mockMvc.perform(post("/students")
                .contentType(MediaType.APPLICATION_JSON)
                .content("{\"name\": \"Jane Doe\", \"email\": \"jane.doe@example.com\"}"))
                .andExpect(status().isCreated())
                .andExpect(jsonPath("$.id").value(1))
                .andExpect(jsonPath("$.name").value("Jane Doe"));
    }
}
```

Explanation:

- **@AutoConfigureMockMvc**: Automatically configures **MockMvc** for testing.
- **@MockBean**: Mocks the StudentService bean, allowing us to simulate its behavior.
- **mockMvc.perform**: Executes a mock HTTP request. Here we simulate a GET and POST request to the /students endpoint.
- **jsonPath**: Asserts the JSON response structure, ensuring the correct values are returned.

Key Considerations for Testing

1. **Test Coverage:** *It is essential to achieve a reasonable and high test coverage, particularly for business-critical code and* APIs.
2. **Mocking:** Focusing on the unit of code under test, Mockito is a good method to Mock dependencies.
3. **Integration Testing:** MockMvc can be leveraged to test the REST APIs without the need to run a full-fledged server, though any complex testing scenarios may presume the use of entire integration tests.
4. **Test Data:** Realistic and context-based test data should be adopted.
5. **Separation of Concerns:** Unit tests are concerned with testing a single module in isolation, whereas integration tests are concerned with testing the interaction between modules.

Conclusion

In this chapter, we explored how to write tests in Spring Boot using **JUnit 5**, **Mockito**, and **MockMvc**. Testing ensures that our application is robust and reliable, providing confidence in its behavior as we build new features.

We've demonstrated:
- How to write unit tests for service classes using **Mockito**.
- How to test REST APIs with **MockMvc**.
- Key best practices and considerations for testing in Spring Boot.

CHAPTER 19

CACHING

In this chapter, we will cover **Caching in Spring Boot**. Caching is an important aspect of improving application performance by storing frequently accessed data in cache memory, which reduces the time-consuming process of repeatedly retrieving data from a database or external API.

We will walk through:
1. Understanding caching in Spring Boot.
2. Using the @Cacheable and @CacheEvict annotations.
3. How to integrate caching with popular providers like **Ehcache** and **Redis**.

What is Caching?

Caching refers to temporarily storing data so that future requests for that data can be served faster. In web applications, caching can be used to store frequently used data, such as query results, computations, or API responses.

Spring Boot provides easy-to-use support for caching, abstracting the underlying implementation so you can focus on business logic while improving performance.

Setting Up Caching in Spring Boot

To enable caching in your Spring Boot application, you need to:

1. Add the required dependencies.
2. Enable caching with the @EnableCaching annotation.
3. Use caching annotations like @Cacheable and @CacheEvict to manage cache operations.

Step 1: Add Dependencies

If you're using **Ehcache** or **Redis** for caching, add the necessary dependencies to your pom.xml.

For **Ehcache**:

```xml
<dependency>
    <groupId>org.springframework.boot</groupId>
    <artifactId>spring-boot-starter-cache</artifactId>
</dependency>

<dependency>
    <groupId>org.ehcache</groupId>
    <artifactId>ehcache</artifactId>
</dependency>
```

For **Redis**:

```xml
<dependency>
    <groupId>org.springframework.boot</groupId>
    <artifactId>spring-boot-starter-cache</artifactId>
</dependency>

<dependency>
    <groupId>org.springframework.boot</groupId>
    <artifactId>spring-boot-starter-data-redis</artifactId>
</dependency>
```

Step 2: Enable Caching

Enable caching in the main application class using the @EnableCaching annotation:

```java
@SpringBootApplication
@EnableCaching
public class StudentApplication {
    public static void main(String[] args) {
        SpringApplication.run(StudentApplication.class, args);
    }
}
```

Step 3. Using @Cacheable and @CacheEvict Annotations

Spring Boot provides two annotations to work with caching:
1. **@Cacheable**: Caches the result of a method call.
2. **@CacheEvict:** Removes data from the cache when the cache is no longer valid.

Using @Cacheable

The @Cacheable annotation is used to indicate that the result of a method can be cached. Let's implement it in the **Student Management API.**

StudentService Class:

```java
@Service
public class StudentService {

    @Autowired
    private StudentRepository studentRepository;

    @Cacheable(value = "students", key = "#id")
    public Student getStudentById(Long id) {
        System.out.println("Fetching student with id " + id);
        return studentRepository.findById(id)
                .orElseThrow(() -> new RuntimeException("Student not found"));
    }
}
```

Explanation:

- value = "students": This specifies the cache name. Here, we're using **"students"** as the cache name.
- key = "#id": This specifies that the cache key will be the **student ID**.

When the getStudentById() method is called with the same id, it will first check if the result is available in the cache. If it is, the cached value is returned; otherwise, the method is executed, and the result is cached.

Using @CacheEvict

The @CacheEvict annotation is used to remove cache entries. It's useful when you update or delete data, and the cache needs to be cleared.

Example

```java
@Service
public class StudentService {

    @Autowired
    private StudentRepository studentRepository;

    @Cacheable(value = "students", key = "#id")
    public Student getStudentById(Long id) {
        return studentRepository.findById(id)
                .orElseThrow(() -> new RuntimeException("Student not found"));
    }

    @CacheEvict(value = "students", key = "#id")
    public void deleteStudent(Long id) {
        studentRepository.deleteById(id);
    }
}
```

Explanation:

- @CacheEvict(value = "students", key = "#id"): Removes the cache entry for the student when deleteStudent() is called.
- Now, if you fetch a student with a deleted ID, it will query the database instead of using cached data.

Integrating with Cache Providers

Spring Boot supports a variety of cache providers like **Ehcache** and **Redis**. Let's look at how to integrate with them.

Integrating with Ehcache

Step 1: Configure Ehcache

First, create an ehcache.xml file to configure Ehcache.

```xml
<config xmlns:xsi="http://www.w3.org/2001/XMLSchema-instance"
        xmlns="http://www.ehcache.org/v3"
        xsi:schemaLocation="http://www.ehcache.org/v3 http://www.ehcache.org/schema/ehcache-core.xsd">

    <cache alias="students">
        <key-type>java.lang.Long</key-type>
        <value-type>com.example.demo.Student</value-type>
        <expiry>
            <ttl unit="minutes">10</ttl>
        </expiry>
        <resources>
            <heap unit="entries">100</heap>
        </resources>
    </cache>
</config>
```

This configuration sets up a cache for students that will store up to 100 entries and expire them after 10 minutes.

Step 2: Configure application.properties

```
spring.cache.jcache.config=classpath:ehcache.xml
```

Integrating with Redis

Step 1: Configure Redis

First, ensure that Redis is installed and running on your local machine or accessible on your server.

Step 2: Configure application.properties

```
spring.redis.host=localhost
spring.redis.port=6379
spring.cache.type=redis
```

This configuration connects your Spring Boot application to the Redis server running on localhost.

Step 3: Use Caching Annotations

The caching annotations (@Cacheable, @CacheEvict) remain the same, as Spring Boot abstracts the underlying cache provider.

Key Considerations for Caching

Here are some best practices to keep in mind when using caching in Spring Boot:

1. **Cache Expiry**: Ensure that cache entries have appropriate expiry times. Stale data can lead to inconsistencies.
2. **Cache Size**: Be mindful of the cache size. Too large a cache can lead to memory issues, especially when using in-memory caches like **Ehcache**.
3. **Choose the Right Cache Provider**: Choose the caching solution that fits your use case. For example, **Redis** is great for distributed caches, while Ehcache is more suitable for local caching.

Conclusion

In this chapter, we explored caching in Spring Boot. We learned how to use the @Cacheable and @CacheEvict annotations to cache method results and clear caches when needed. We also integrated Spring Boot with two popular cache providers: **Ehcache** and **Redis**.

Caching is a powerful tool to improve the performance of your Spring Boot applications, but it's essential to use it wisely and monitor its impact on your system.

CHAPTER 20

MESSAGING: INTEGRATING KAFKA AND RABBITMQ

Message brokers are important in modern applications as well as microservice-based architectures. These platforms simplify communication and make it possible for services to communicate in a scalable and a loosely-coupled manner. Among the most popular messaging brokers are **Apache Kafka** and **RabbitMQ** and both are well supported with Spring Boot out of the box.

In this chapter, you will be introduced to **message-driven architectures** and also learn to incorporate Kafka and RabbitMQ into a Spring Boot project.

What is a Message-Driven Architecture?

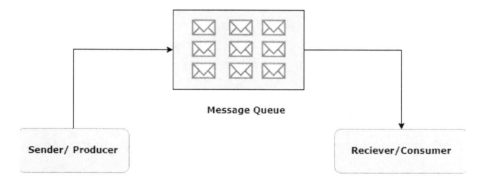

A **message-driven architecture** is best exemplified by a system design where an intermediary message broker allows for asynchronous communication by its services through messages. Instead of calling services directly, a system sends a message to a broker that queues up the services needed to process that message.

Benefits of Message-Driven Architecture:

- **Loose Coupling**: Services are not tightly coupled because they do not call each other directly.
- **Scalability**: Services can be scaled out independently, which helps improve load balancing.
- **Fault Tolerance**: When a certain service is unavailable, all messages will persist in some queue until the service comes back up.
- **Asynchronous Processing**: A task may be performed in the background without the end-user noticing it.

Why Use Kafka or RabbitMQ?

Kafka:

- Kafka is best applied in cases where efficient and reliable real-time data streaming is required, especially in media applications.
- It finds its usage for example in event-based architecture where it receives and sends millions of messages every second.

RabbitMQ:

- RabbitMQ is ideal for complex routing, ensuring **reliable message delivery,** and handling various messaging patterns like **publish/subscribe** and **request/reply**.
- It is widely used for tasks that require **robust message guarantees**, such as processing financial transactions.

Integrating Spring Boot with Apache Kafka

Let's now put together everything we have said by focusing on how to connect Spring Boot to Apache Kafka. In this mode of operation, the producer pushes the messages to topics and the consumer pulls the messages from topics.

Step 1: Add Kafka Dependencies

To get started with Kafka, include the following dependency in your pom.xml file:

```xml
<dependency>
    <groupId>org.springframework.boot</groupId>
    <artifactId>spring-boot-starter-kafka</artifactId>
</dependency>
```

Step 2: Kafka Configuration

Configure Kafka in your application.properties file to define the Kafka broker and consumer group settings:

```
spring.kafka.bootstrap-servers=localhost:9092
spring.kafka.consumer.group-id=group_id
spring.kafka.consumer.auto-offset-reset=earliest
```

- **bootstrap-servers**: Specifies the Kafka server address.
- **group-id**: Defines the consumer group, allowing multiple consumers to share the work.
- **auto-offset-reset**: Tells Kafka where to start reading messages when no initial offset is available.

Step 3: Kafka Producer Example

In Kafka, producers send messages to topics. Let's implement a simple Kafka producer that sends messages to a topic called studentTopic:

```java
import org.springframework.kafka.core.KafkaTemplate;
import org.springframework.beans.factory.annotation.Autowired;
import org.springframework.web.bind.annotation.*;

@RestController
@RequestMapping("/kafka")
public class KafkaProducerController {

    @Autowired
    private KafkaTemplate<String, String> kafkaTemplate;

    private static final String TOPIC = "studentTopic";

    @PostMapping("/publish/{message}")
    public String sendMessageToKafka(@PathVariable("message") final String message) {
        kafkaTemplate.send(TOPIC, message);
        return "Message sent to Kafka Topic!";
    }
}
```

Explanation:

- The KafkaTemplate object is used to send messages to the Kafka topic.
- Thesend() method sends the provided message to the topic studentTopic.

Step 4: Kafka Consumer Example

Now, let's implement a **Kafka Consumer** to receive and process the messages sent by the producer:

```java
import org.springframework.kafka.annotation.KafkaListener;
import org.springframework.stereotype.Service;

@Service
public class KafkaConsumer {

    @KafkaListener(topics = "studentTopic", groupId = "group_id")
    public void consumeMessage(String message) {
        System.out.println("Consumed message: " + message);
    }
}
```

Explanation:

- The @KafkaListener annotation tells Spring Boot that this method will listen to the studentTopic for messages.
- Once a message is received, it is printed to the console.

Integrating Spring Boot with RabbitMQ

RabbitMQ is another popular message broker that follows the **publish/subscribe** and **message queue** models. Let's look at how to integrate RabbitMQ with Spring Boot.

Step 1: Add RabbitMQ Dependencies

To integrate RabbitMQ with Spring Boot, include the following dependency in your pom.xml file:

```xml
<dependency>
    <groupId>org.springframework.boot</groupId>
    <artifactId>spring-boot-starter-amqp</artifactId>
</dependency>
```

Step 2: RabbitMQ Configuration

In your application.properties, configure RabbitMQ settings as follows:

```
spring.rabbitmq.host=localhost
spring.rabbitmq.port=5672
spring.rabbitmq.username=guest
spring.rabbitmq.password=guest
```

Step 3: RabbitMQ Producer Example

RabbitMQ producers send messages to exchanges, which then route the messages to queues based on bindings. Here's an example of a RabbitMQ producer:

```java
import org.springframework.amqp.rabbit.core.RabbitTemplate;
import org.springframework.beans.factory.annotation.Autowired;
import org.springframework.web.bind.annotation.*;

@RestController
@RequestMapping("/rabbitmq")
public class RabbitMQProducerController {

    @Autowired
    private RabbitTemplate rabbitTemplate;

    private static final String EXCHANGE = "studentExchange";
    private static final String ROUTING_KEY = "studentRoutingKey";

    @PostMapping("/publish/{message}")
    public String sendMessageToRabbitMQ(@PathVariable("message") String message) {
        rabbitTemplate.convertAndSend(EXCHANGE, ROUTING_KEY, message);
        return "Message sent to RabbitMQ!";
    }
}
```

Explanation:

- **RabbitTemplate** is used to send messages to the studentExchange.
- The convertAndSend() method sends the message to the exchange, which is routed using the studentRoutingKey.

Step 4: RabbitMQ Consumer Example

Let's implement a **RabbitMQ Consumer** to process messages from a queue:

```java
@Service
public class RabbitMQConsumer {

    @RabbitListener(queues = "studentQueue")
    public void consumeMessageFromQueue(String message) {
        System.out.println("Consumed message from RabbitMQ: " + message);
    }
}
```

Explanation:

- The @RabbitListener annotation listens for messages on the studentQueue and processes them when they arrive.

Step 5: RabbitMQ Configuration Class

In RabbitMQ, we need to define exchanges, queues, and bindings using a configuration class:

```java
import org.springframework.amqp.core.*;
import org.springframework.context.annotation.Bean;
import org.springframework.context.annotation.Configuration;

@Configuration
public class RabbitMQConfig {

    @Bean
    public TopicExchange studentExchange() {
        return new TopicExchange("studentExchange");
    }

    @Bean
    public Queue studentQueue() {
        return new Queue("studentQueue");
    }

    @Bean
    public Binding binding(Queue queue, TopicExchange exchange) {
        return BindingBuilder.bind(queue).to(exchange).with("studentRoutingKey");
    }
}
```

Explanation:

- The TopicExchange routes messages to different queues based on routing keys.
- The Queue represents where the messages will be stored.
- The Binding defines how the exchange will route the messages to the queue.

Monitoring and Best Practices

Both **Kafka** and **RabbitMQ** offer built-in tools for monitoring queues, message throughput, and performance metrics. You can also integrate with **Spring Boot Actuator** to expose key metrics via endpoints.

Key Considerations:

- **Message Durability**: Enable message persistence to avoid data loss.
- **Acknowledgments**: Ensure proper message acknowledgment to guarantee reliable delivery.
- **Error Handling**: Use retries and dead-letter queues to handle failed messages.

Conclusion

In this chapter, we explored how to integrate **Kafka** and **RabbitMQ** with Spring Boot, providing examples of both producers and consumers. Messaging systems like Kafka and RabbitMQ are powerful tools for building **scalable, fault-tolerant**, and **asynchronous** applications.

By now, you should have a solid understanding of how to implement messaging in a Spring Boot application, whether you're building real-time data streaming with Kafka or reliable messaging systems with RabbitMQ.

CHAPTER 21

DEPLOYING APPLICATIONS

Spring Boot makes the process of writing Java applications straightforward, but once you create an application, the next challenge is making sure it is deployed and users can get to interact with it. In this chapter, we will address some steps that one can follow to deploy Spring Boot applications and also integrate them with **AWS** and **Azure** — how to make their JARs or WARs and how to install them on these popular platforms.

Packaging Spring Boot Applications: JAR vs. WAR

1. JAR (Java ARchive)

By default, Spring Boot applications use executable JARs for packaging. Compiled Java code along with all the dependencies is included in a JAR file. The great thing about this is that the JAR file, in essence, does not need any external servlet container (like Tomcat) to be able to work since the JAR file is self-sustaining.

How to Package a Spring Boot Application as a JAR

Out of the box Spring Boot has JAR file packaging capabilities for the applications. It is as simple as running the command below using **Maven** or **Gradle**:

For Maven:

```
mvn clean package
```

For Gradle:

```
./gradlew build
```

Once the build process completes, you'll find the executable JAR in the target/ directory (for Maven) or build/libs/ (for Gradle).

You can run your application with the following command:

```
java -jar target/myapp-0.0.1-SNAPSHOT.jar
```

The application will start up, and you can access it via http://localhost:8080.

2. WAR (Web Application Archive)

In certain instances, an external servlet container such as Tomcat or Jetty may be necessary for the deployment of your Spring Boot application. In this case, it is mandatory to package the application in a WAR file..

How to Package a Spring Boot Application as a WAR

1. Update your pom.xml to include the necessary dependencies:

```xml
<packaging>war</packaging>
<dependency>
    <groupId>org.springframework.boot</groupId>
    <artifactId>spring-boot-starter-tomcat</artifactId>
    <scope>provided</scope>
</dependency>
```

2. Modify the SpringBootApplication class to extend SpringBootServletInitializer:

```
import org.springframework.boot.builder.SpringApplicationBuilder;
import org.springframework.boot.web.servlet.support.SpringBootServletInitializer;

@SpringBootApplication
public class MyApplication extends SpringBootServletInitializer {

    @Override
    protected SpringApplicationBuilder configure(SpringApplicationBuilder application) {
        return application.sources(MyApplication.class);
    }

    public static void main(String[] args) {
        SpringApplication.run(MyApplication.class, args);
    }
}
```

3. Build the application:

```
mvn clean package
```

This will generate a WAR file in the target/ directory that can be deployed to an external servlet container.

Deploying to Cloud Platforms

The packaging being done in the previous stage is followed by deploying the Spring Boot application in the cloud. Now we can see how a Spring Boot application can be deployed in AWS and Azure Cloud.

Deploying to AWS (Amazon Web Services)

Option 1: Deploying on Elastic Beanstalk

AWS Elastic Beanstalk is a managed service that makes it easy to deploy and scale Spring Boot applications in the cloud.

1.Create an Elastic Beanstalk Application:

- Sign in to your AWS console and navigate to **Elastic Beanstalk**.
- Click on **Create a new environment** and select **Web Server Environment**.
- Choose **Java** as the platform.

2. Deploy Your JAR/WAR File:

- Upload your packaged JAR or WAR file (from the target/ directory) to the environment.
- Elastic Beanstalk will automatically provision the infrastructure and deploy your application.

3. Access Your Application:

- Once deployed, AWS will provide you with a public URL for accessing your application.

Option 2: Deploying to EC2

You can also deploy your Spring Boot application directly to an **EC2 instance:**

1.Launch an EC2 Instance:

Create an EC2 instance and SSH into it.

2. Install Java:

Ensure that Java is installed on the instance by running:

```
sudo apt-get install openjdk-11-jdk
```

3. Transfer Your JAR File:

Use scp to transfer the JAR file to the EC2 instance:

```
scp target/myapp-0.0.1-SNAPSHOT.jar ec2-user@<EC2-IP-ADDRESS>:/home/ec2-user/
```

4. Run the Application:

SSH into your EC2 instance and run the application:

```
java -jar myapp-0.0.1-SNAPSHOT.jar
```

Deploying to Microsoft Azure

Azure App Service provides a fully managed platform for deploying Spring Boot applications.

1.Create an App Service:

- Go to the **Azure Portal** and create a new **App Service**.
- Select **Java 11** as the runtime stack.

2. Deploy Your Application:

- Upload your JAR/WAR file using **FTP**, **Git**, or the **Azure CLI**:

```
az webapp deployment source config-zip - resource-group myResourceGroup - name myApp - src
target/myapp-0.0.1-SNAPSHOT.jar
```

3. Access Your Application:

- Azure will provide a public URL to access your deployed Spring Boot application.

Best Practices for Deploying Spring Boot Applications

- **Environment-Specific Configuration**: Use Spring Boot **profiles** (dev, test, prod) to configure your application for different environments. You can define specific properties in application-dev.properties, application-prod.properties, etc.
- **Externalized Configuration**: Sensitive information, for example, credentials to the database, should not be embedded in the code and should be stored outside, in files, or environment variables.

- **Monitoring and Logging**: Using Spring Boot Actuator it is possible to expose health and metrics endpoints, Expose them in production settings being important for your application management.
- **Scaling**: You need to have auto-scaling, deployment platforms and features especially where you expect a heavy load. For instance, AWS Elastic Beanstalk and Azure App service automatically scale according to the load.

Conclusion

It is just a matter of packaging your application either in a JAR or WAR file. Application hosting in the cloud with providers such as AWS, Azure, and Heroku means you can deploy your applications almost instantly and easily scale them. In addition, learning such deployment techniques and practices will help you in creating real-world Spring Boot applications that are reliable, scalable, and easy to maintain.

CHAPTER 22

SERVICE DISCOVERY AND API GATEWAY

Application development through microservice architecture has gained popularity for the creation of large systems with easy scalability. The microservices allow for independent development, deployment, and scaling of each application part. In this chapter, we will consider the key elements of building a microservices-based architecture on Spring Boot, namely, the **Eureka service registry** and the **Zuul API gateway**.

What is a Microservices Architecture?

Microservices architecture is a business strategy in software development where the application is divided into groups of small, self-contained, and looped services. Each service is accompanied by strong functional qualities that allow it to function independently of other services in the micro-system and can be effectively expanded, launched, or deployed on their own.

The following are some of the advantages offered by microservices:
1. **Scalability**: Services can be scaled across the board according to user requirements without straining other elements in the structure.
2. **Fault Isolation**: One service may fail without causing the entire network to be down, exemplifying redundancy in communication.
3. **Independent Deployment**: Services can be updated without affecting other parts of the system.
4. **Technology Diversity**: This allows the adoption of a variety of technologies that may be appropriate for particular tasks.

In a Spring Boot microservices architecture, Spring Cloud offers tools for the common aspects of microservices, including service registration and discovery, load balancing, and centralized configuration, among others.

Key Components in Microservices Architecture

1. **Service Discovery**: Microservices need a mechanism for finding other microservices. In real-time, Eureka acts as a service registry that monitors the whereabouts of services.
2. **API Gateway**: An API Gateway is a point of entry to the microservices, which performs request routing, authentication, and rate limiting operations. Zuul is said to be an API Gateway in the Spring Cloud microservices.

Setting Up the Project

To start, we'll set up three Spring Boot projects:
1. **Eureka Server** — Acts as the service registry.
2. **API Gateway with Zuul** — Routes requests to different microservices.
3. **Microservices** — Example services that will register with Eureka and communicate via the API Gateway.

Service Discovery with Eureka

Eureka is a REST-based service registry provided by Netflix. Microservices register with Eureka and can locate other registered services without knowing their exact URLs.

Setting Up Eureka Server

1.Create a Eureka Server Project:

In your pom.xml, add the Eureka Server dependency:

```
<dependency>
    <groupId>org.springframework.cloud</groupId>
    <artifactId>spring-cloud-starter-netflix-eureka-server</artifactId>
</dependency>
```

2. Enable Eureka Server:

In the main application class, annotate it with @EnableEurekaServer:

```
@SpringBootApplication
@EnableEurekaServer
public class EurekaServerApplication {
    public static void main(String[] args) {
        SpringApplication.run(EurekaServerApplication.class, args);
    }
}
```

3. Application Properties:

Configure the Eureka Server in application.properties:

```
server.port=8761
eureka.client.register-with-eureka=false
eureka.client.fetch-registry=false
```

4. Run Eureka Server:

Start the application, and Eureka will run on port 8761. The Eureka dashboard can be accessed at http://localhost:8761.

Registering a Microservice with Eureka

Next, let's create a microservice (e.g., a **StudentService**) and register it with Eureka.

1.Add Eureka Client Dependency:

In the pom.xml of your microservice, add the Eureka client dependency:

```
<dependency>
    <groupId>org.springframework.cloud</groupId>
    <artifactId>spring-cloud-starter-netflix-eureka-client</artifactId>
</dependency>
```

2. Enable Eureka Client:

In the main application class, add @EnableEurekaClient:

```
@SpringBootApplication
@EnableEurekaClient
public class StudentServiceApplication {
    public static void main(String[] args) {
        SpringApplication.run(StudentServiceApplication.class, args);
    }
}
```

3. Application Properties:

Add the following to register with Eureka:

```
server.port=8081
spring.application.name=student-service
eureka.client.service-url.defaultZone=http://localhost:8761/eureka
```

4. Creating an Example Endpoint:

Start the application, and Eureka will run on port 8761. The Eureka dashboard can be accessed at http://localhost:8761.

Registering a Microservice with Eureka

Add a REST controller to verify the service is running:

```
@RestController
@RequestMapping("/students")
public class StudentController {

    @GetMapping("/{id}")
    public String getStudentById(@PathVariable("id") Long id) {
        return "Student with ID " + id;
    }
}
```

Now, start the Student Service, and it will automatically register with the Eureka server.

API Gateway with Zuul

An **API Gateway** provides a unified entry point for clients to interact with multiple services. **Zuul** is a popular API Gateway provided by Netflix that handles routing and filters requests to various backend services.

Setting Up Zuul API Gateway

1.Create a Zuul Gateway Project:

In your pom.xml, add the Zuul and Eureka client dependencies:

```xml
<dependency>
    <groupId>org.springframework.cloud</groupId>
    <artifactId>spring-cloud-starter-netflix-zuul</artifactId>
</dependency>
<dependency>
    <groupId>org.springframework.cloud</groupId>
    <artifactId>spring-cloud-starter-netflix-eureka-client</artifactId>
</dependency>
```

2. Enable Zuul Proxy:

In the main application class, add @EnableZuulProxy and @EnableEurekaClient:

```java
@SpringBootApplication
@EnableZuulProxy
@EnableEurekaClient
public class ApiGatewayApplication {
    public static void main(String[] args) {
        SpringApplication.run(ApiGatewayApplication.class, args);
    }
}
```

3. Application Properties:

Configure Zuul in application.properties:

```
server.port=8762
eureka.client.service-url.defaultZone=http://localhost:8761/eureka
```

4. Routing with Zuul:

Zuul automatically routes requests based on service names registered in Eureka. For example, student-service requests can be accessed via:

```
http://localhost:8762/student-service/students/{id}
```

You can also implement an API gateway using Spring Cloud Gateway. Learn in detail here.

Testing the Setup

1. **Start the Eureka Server, Zuul Gateway, and Student Service**.
2. **Access the Eureka Dashboard**: Visit http://localhost:8761 to view registered services.
3. **Testing the Gateway**: Access the Student Service via Zuul by visiting:

```
http://localhost:8762/student-service/students/1
```

Zuul will route the request to the Student Service, and the response should display:

```
Student with ID 1
```

This setup demonstrates how Eureka and Zuul work together in a microservices environment.

Zuul routes requests to the appropriate service instance based on the Eureka service registry, providing a seamless API gateway.

Conclusion

The building blocks of an ecosystem powered by Spring Boot microservices architecture with microservice Eureka and API gateway Zuul were outlined in this article. The service registry Eureka simplifies service broadcasting, while the API gateway Zuul simplifies the routing and filtering of requests. With these components together, the architecture of microservices is made scalable, resilient, and easier to maintain.

This type of infrastructure will provide a base for growing a microservices application where other components of Spring Cloud will be included such as circuit breakers (**Resilience4j**) and centralized control over the configuration (**Spring Cloud Config**), hence this type of microservice application is very scalable and can be used in production.

CHAPTER 23

SPRING CLOUD AND DISTRIBUTED SYSTEMS

In today's digital landscape, microservices architecture has gained prominence in modern-day software applications. In this chapter, we are going to discuss the fundamental concepts and components of Spring Cloud, which include service registration, load balancing, circuit breaking, and configuration management. The concepts will be more practical, and we will include code snippets illustrating how they can be implemented.

Why Use Spring Cloud for Microservices?

Spring Cloud solutions resolve several problems that come along with implementing a microservices architecture, for instance:

- **Service Discovery and Registration**: Provides a way through which each service can dynamically find and talk to all the other services without the need for hardcoded endpoints.

- **Load Balancing**: It allows requests to be distributed evenly among the numerous instances of one service.

- **Circuit Breakers**: Implements a way of isolating faults by shutting service circuits that are unresponsive.

- **Centralized Configuration**: Enables configuration policy enforcement across microservices to reduce redundant and inconsistent configurations.

With these capabilities, Spring Cloud helps developers build fault-tolerant systems that are easier to scale and maintain.

Getting Started: Setting Up Spring Cloud

Now, before we get into concrete use cases, let's create a Spring Cloud project. For this, we will use **Spring Cloud dependencies** within a Spring Boot application.

1. Add Spring Cloud Dependencies:

```xml
<dependencyManagement>
    <dependencies>
        <dependency>
            <groupId>org.springframework.cloud</groupId>
            <artifactId>spring-cloud-dependencies</artifactId>
            <version>2021.0.5</version>
            <type>pom</type>
            <scope>import</scope>
        </dependency>
    </dependencies>
</dependencyManagement>

<dependencies>
    <dependency>
        <groupId>org.springframework.cloud</groupId>
        <artifactId>spring-cloud-starter-netflix-eureka-server</artifactId>
    </dependency>
    <dependency>
        <groupId>org.springframework.cloud</groupId>
        <artifactId>spring-cloud-starter-netflix-eureka-client</artifactId>
    </dependency>
    <dependency>
        <groupId>org.springframework.cloud</groupId>
        <artifactId>spring-cloud-starter-openfeign</artifactId>
    </dependency>
    <dependency>
        <groupId>org.springframework.cloud</groupId>
        <artifactId>spring-cloud-starter-circuitbreaker-resilience4j</artifactId>
    </dependency>
</dependencies>
```

Here, we're including dependencies for **Eureka** (for service discovery), **Feign** (for inter-service communication), and **Resilience4j** (for circuit breaking).

2. Configure Spring Cloud in Application Properties:

```
spring.application.name=my-microservice
eureka.client.service-url.defaultZone=http://localhost:8761/eureka
```

Service Discovery with Eureka

Eureka is a service registry where each microservice registers itself and retrieves the locations of other services.

Setting Up Eureka Server

1.Create a New Project for the Eureka Server.

2.Add the Eureka Server Dependency:

```
<dependency>
    <groupId>org.springframework.cloud</groupId>
    <artifactId>spring-cloud-starter-netflix-eureka-server</artifactId>
</dependency>
```

3. Enable Eureka Server: In the main application class, annotate with @EnableEurekaServer:

```
@SpringBootApplication
@EnableEurekaServer
public class EurekaServerApplication {
    public static void main(String[] args) {
        SpringApplication.run(EurekaServerApplication.class, args);
    }
}
```

4. Application Properties:

```
server.port=8761
eureka.client.register-with-eureka=false
eureka.client.fetch-registry=false
```

Run the server, and it will start on the port 8761.

Registering Microservices with Eureka

In your other microservices, add the Eureka client dependency and enable the Eureka client in the main application class.

```
@SpringBootApplication
@EnableEurekaClient
public class MyServiceApplication {
    public static void main(String[] args) {
        SpringApplication.run(MyServiceApplication.class, args);
    }
}
```

Each service will automatically register itself with the Eureka server, making it discoverable by other services.

Inter-Service Communication with Feign

Feign provides a declarative REST client for Spring Boot, making it easier to communicate between microservices.

Using Feign to Communicate Between Services

1. **Add Feign Client Annotation**: Create an interface for the client and annotate it with @FeignClient:

```
@FeignClient(name = "student-service")
public interface StudentClient {
@GetMapping("/students/{id}")
  Student getStudentById(@PathVariable Long id);
}
```

2. Enable Feign in Application: In the main application class, add the @EnableFeignClients annotation:

```
@SpringBootApplication
@EnableFeignClients
public class MyServiceApplication {
    public static void main(String[] args) {
        SpringApplication.run(MyServiceApplication.class, args);
    }
}
```

Now, the service can use the StudentClient interface to interact with the student-service microservice. Feign handles the HTTP request and response conversion automatically.

Load Balancing with Ribbon

Ribbon performs automatic load balancing between the instances of services that are registered with **EUREKA**. When using Spring Cloud, Feign has integrated into Ribbon automatically.

1. **Add Multiple Instances in Eureka**: Ribbon will automatically find them if multiple instances of an application are registered on Eureka.
2. **Load Balancing Requests**: if a user performs requests using Feign's functionality Ribbon will balance the requests towards the available instances.

This setup ensures that our application remains scalable, distributing requests evenly among instances.

Circuit Breaking with Resilience4j

Circuit breakers prevent cascading failures by breaking circuits when a service becomes unresponsive. Here, we'll use **Resilience4j** with Feign.

1. **Add Resilience4j Annotations**: In your Feign client, use the @CircuitBreaker annotation:

```
@CircuitBreaker(name = "studentService", fallbackMethod = "fallbackStudentById")
public Student getStudentById(@PathVariable Long id);

public Student fallbackStudentById(Long id, Throwable throwable) {
    return new Student(id, "Fallback", "Student");
}
```

If student-service becomes unavailable, the fallbackStudentById method will return a fallback response.

2. Configuration: You can configure circuit breaker settings in application.properties:

```
resilience4j.circuitbreaker.instances.studentService.slidingWindowSize=10
resilience4j.circuitbreaker.instances.studentService.failureRateThreshold=50
```

This setup improves system resilience by ensuring that failures in one service don't affect others.

Centralized Configuration with Spring Cloud Config

Spring Cloud Config allows you to manage configuration properties for multiple microservices in a centralized manner.

Setting Up a Config Server

1.Create a New Project for Config Server:

2.Add the Spring Cloud Config Dependency:

3. Enable Config Server: In the main application class, add the @EnableConfigServer annotation:

```
@SpringBootApplication
@EnableConfigServer
public class ConfigServerApplication {
    public static void main(String[] args) {
        SpringApplication.run(ConfigServerApplication.class, args);
    }
}
```

4. Configure Properties:

```
spring.cloud.config.server.git.uri=https://github.com/your-repo/config-repo
```

Config Client Setup

Add the Spring Cloud Config client dependency to your microservices:

```
<dependency>
    <groupId>org.springframework.cloud</groupId>
    <artifactId>spring-cloud-starter-config</artifactId>
</dependency>
```

Set the spring.config.name and spring.cloud.config.uri in each microservice's application.properties.

Conclusion

Spring Cloud enables the realization of the basic features of microservices architecture including service discovery, load balancing, circuit breaking, and centralized configuration. With such tools, developers can concentrate on creating seamless, fluid, and easy-to-maintainable applications. After learning how each fundamental feature can be implemented with code examples, you're now properly prepared to create powerful and diverse distributed systems with Spring Cloud.

CHAPTER 24

SPRING BOOT WITH GRAPHQL

GraphQL is a powerful tool that enables flexible and efficient data retrieval in modern applications. In this chapter, we'll introduce GraphQL, explore why it's beneficial, and guide you through building a **GraphQL API** in **Spring Boot**. We'll continue with our **Student Management API** example for consistency, implementing GraphQL features step-by-step.

What is GraphQL?

GraphQL is a query language for APIs and a runtime for executing those queries by fetching only the data you need. Created by Facebook, GraphQL allows clients to request specific fields from APIs, providing flexibility and efficiency compared to REST.

Why Use GraphQL?

1. **Flexible Data Retrieval**: With GraphQL, clients specify exactly what data they need, making responses more efficient.
2. **Reduced Over-fetching and Under-fetching**: In REST APIs, clients may receive extra data or miss necessary information. GraphQL eliminates this problem by allowing selective data requests.
3. **Single Endpoint**: Instead of multiple endpoints for different data, GraphQL uses a single endpoint for all queries and mutations.
4. **Strongly Typed Schema**: GraphQL uses a schema to define types and structure, ensuring predictable responses.

Setting Up Spring Boot with GraphQL

To start, we'll create a **GraphQL API** that supports queries and mutations for our **Student Management** system. Here's how to integrate GraphQL with Spring Boot:

1. Add Dependencies

In the pom.xml, add dependencies for **Spring Boot**, **GraphQL**, and **GraphQL Java Tools**:

```xml
<dependency>
    <groupId>com.graphql-java-kickstart</groupId>
    <artifactId>graphql-spring-boot-starter</artifactId>
    <version>11.1.0</version>
</dependency>
<dependency>
    <groupId>com.graphql-java-kickstart</groupId>
    <artifactId>graphiql-spring-boot-starter</artifactId>
    <version>11.1.0</version>
</dependency>
<dependency>
    <groupId>org.springframework.boot</groupId>
    <artifactId>spring-boot-starter-data-jpa</artifactId>
</dependency>
<dependency>
    <groupId>org.springframework.boot</groupId>
    <artifactId>spring-boot-starter-web</artifactId>
</dependency>
<dependency>
    <groupId>com.h2database</groupId>
    <artifactId>h2</artifactId>
    <scope>runtime</scope>
</dependency>
```

2. Define the GraphQL Schema

GraphQL uses a **schema** to define data structure and queries. In our project's resources folder, create a file called schema.graphqls.

```
type Query {
    studentById(id: ID!): Student
    allStudents: [Student]
}

type Mutation {
    createStudent(name: String!, age: Int!): Student
    updateStudent(id: ID!, name: String, age: Int): Student
    deleteStudent(id: ID!): String
}

type Student {
    id: ID!
    name: String!
    age: Int!
}
```

This schema defines:

- **Query** for fetching individual or all students. Query type is used for operations that fetch the information.
- **Mutation** for creating, updating, and deleting students. Mutation type is used for writing the information.
- **Student** type with id, name, and age fields.

3. Create the Student Entity

Define the Student entity that maps to a database table.

```
@Entity
public class Student {

    @Id
    @GeneratedValue(strategy = GenerationType.IDENTITY)
    private Long id;
```

```
    private String name;
    private int age;
    // Getters and Setters
}
```

4. Build the Repository Layer

Create a StudentRepository interface for managing CRUD operations.

```java
import org.springframework.data.jpa.repository.JpaRepository;

public interface StudentRepository extends JpaRepository<Student, Long> {
}
```

5. Implement Service Logic

Our service will handle the business logic for student management.

```java
@Service
public class StudentService {

    @Autowired
    private StudentRepository studentRepository;

    public List<Student> getAllStudents() {
        return studentRepository.findAll();
    }
}
```

```java
public Student createStudent(String name, int age) {
    Student student = new Student();
    student.setName(name);
    student.setAge(age);
    return studentRepository.save(student);
}

public Student updateStudent(Long id, String name, int age) {
    Optional<Student> studentOpt = studentRepository.findById(id);
    if (studentOpt.isPresent()) {
        Student student = studentOpt.get();
        if (name != null) student.setName(name);
        if (age != 0) student.setAge(age);
        return studentRepository.save(student);
    }
    return null;
}

public String deleteStudent(Long id) {
    studentRepository.deleteById(id);
    return "Student deleted successfully";
}
}
```

6. Define GraphQL Resolver Classes

Resolvers define how to fetch data for each field in the GraphQL schema.

Query Resolver

The Query Resolver handles fetching data. Implement studentById and allStudents.

```java
import com.coxautodev.graphql.tools.GraphQLQueryResolver;
import org.springframework.beans.factory.annotation.Autowired;
import org.springframework.stereotype.Component;
import java.util.List;

@Component
public class StudentQueryResolver implements GraphQLQueryResolver {

    @Autowired
    private StudentService studentService;

    public Student studentById(Long id) {
        return studentService.getStudentById(id).orElse(null);
    }

    public List<Student> allStudents() {
        return studentService.getAllStudents();
    }
}
```

Mutation Resolver

The Mutation Resolver handles creating, updating, and deleting data.

```java
@Component
public class StudentMutationResolver implements GraphQLMutationResolver {

    @Autowired
    private StudentService studentService;

    public Student createStudent(String name, int age) {
        return studentService.createStudent(name, age);
    }

    public Student updateStudent(Long id, String name, int age) {
        return studentService.updateStudent(id, name, age);
    }

    public String deleteStudent(Long id) {
        return studentService.deleteStudent(id);
    }
}
```

7. Testing GraphQL Queries and Mutations

To test, run the Spring Boot application and open <u>The Mutation Resolver handles creating, updating, and deleting data.</u> to access GraphiQL, an in-browser GraphQL IDE.

Query Examples

1.Fetch All Students:

```
query {
    allStudents {
        id
        name
        age
    }
}
```

2. Fetch a Student by ID:

```
query {
    studentById(id: 1) {
        id
        name
        age
    }
}
```

Query Examples

1.Create a New Student:

```
mutation {
    createStudent(name: "Alice", age: 20) {
        id
        name
        age
    }
}
```

2. Update an Existing Student:

```
mutation {
    updateStudent(id: 1, name: "Alice Updated", age: 21) {
        id
        name
        age
    }
}
```

3. Delete a Student:

```
mutation {
        deleteStudent(id: 1)
}
```

Conclusion

In this chapter, we explored how to integrate **GraphQL** with **Spring Boot** for our **Student Management API**. We learned the basics of GraphQL, set up queries and mutations, and tested everything in GraphiQL. GraphQL's flexibility allows clients to query only the necessary data, optimizing bandwidth and performance. Spring Boot's integration with GraphQL provides a powerful way to build modern, efficient APIs.

With this, our Spring Boot application is now equipped with GraphQL, enhancing the way we interact with our data! Continue exploring more advanced GraphQL features, like **filtering, sorting,** and **pagination**, to further optimize your application.

CHAPTER 25

SPRING BOOT WITH GRPC

In this chapter, we'll dive into **gRPC** — an efficient, high-performance RPC (Remote Procedure Call) framework. We'll explore why gRPC is worth considering, especially for building microservices in Spring Boot, and how to implement it in our **Student Management API** example.

What is gRPC?

gRPC (Google Remote Procedure Call) is an open-source RPC framework developed by Google, enabling microservices to communicate with each other across different languages and environments. Some key advantages of gRPC include:

- **High Performance**: Uses HTTP/2 and Protobuf, making it faster than JSON-based REST APIs.
- **Streaming**: Supports client-side, server-side, and bi-directional streaming.
- **Multi-Language Support**: gRPC can work across multiple languages, making it versatile.

Why Use gRPC in Spring Boot?

For applications that rely heavily on inter-service communication, **gRPC** can improve performance over traditional REST APIs by compressing data with a binary protocol. Here's why you should consider using it in Spring Boot microservices:

- **Speed**: Fast communication due to Protobuf serialization and HTTP/2.
- **Efficiency**: gRPC reduces bandwidth by using binary payloads.
- **Better Suitability for Microservices**: Efficient for both request-response and streaming operations.

Setting Up gRPC with Spring Boot

To use gRPC with Spring Boot, follow these steps:

1. **Add Dependencies**: Set up your Spring Boot project to support gRPC and Protobuf.
2. **Define Protobuf Schema**: Define your data model and methods.
3. **Generate gRPC Classes**: Use Maven or Gradle to generate gRPC classes.
4. **Implement Server**: Build the gRPC server within Spring Boot.
5. **Create Client**: Set up a client to call your gRPC service.

Step 1: Adding Dependencies

Add the following dependencies in your pom.xml file to enable gRPC in Spring Boot:

```xml
<dependency>
    <groupId>net.devh</groupId>
    <artifactId>grpc-spring-boot-starter</artifactId>
    <version>2.13.0.RELEASE</version>
</dependency>
<dependency>
    <groupId>com.google.protobuf</groupId>
    <artifactId>protobuf-java</artifactId>
    <version>3.19.1</version>
</dependency>
<dependency>
    <groupId>io.grpc</groupId>
    <artifactId>grpc-netty</artifactId>
    <version>1.40.1</version>
</dependency>
```

Step 2: Define the Protobuf Schema

Let's define our **Student Management API** methods in a .proto file. Create a file named student.proto in the src/main/proto directory.

```proto
syntax = "proto3";

option java_package = "com.example.student.grpc";
option java_outer_classname = "StudentServiceProto";

service StudentService {
    rpc GetStudentInfo (StudentRequest) returns (StudentResponse);
    rpc AddStudent (NewStudentRequest) returns (StudentResponse);
}

message StudentRequest {
    int32 id = 1;
}

message NewStudentRequest {
    string name = 1;
    int32 age = 2;
    string course = 3;
}

message StudentResponse {
    int32 id = 1;
    string name = 2;
    int32 age = 3;
    string course = 4;
}
```

Step 3: Generating gRPC Classes

To generate Java classes from the Protobuf schema, add the Protobuf plugin to your Maven or Gradle configuration:

In Maven:

```xml
<build>
    <plugins>
        <plugin>
            <groupId>org.xolstice.maven.plugins</groupId>
            <artifactId>protobuf-maven-plugin</artifactId>
            <version>0.6.1</version>
            <configuration>

<protocArtifact>com.google.protobuf:protoc:3.19.1:exe:${os.detected.classifier}</protocArtifact>
            </configuration>
            <executions>
                <execution>
                    <goals>
                        <goal>compile</goal>
                        <goal>compile-custom</goal>
                    </goals>
                </execution>
            </executions>
        </plugin>
    </plugins>
</build>
```

Run mvn compile to generate Java classes for your Protobuf files.

Step 4: Implementing the gRPC Server

Create a service that implements the StudentServiceGrpc.StudentServiceImplBase class generated from the Protobuf file.

```java
@Service
public class StudentServiceImpl extends StudentServiceGrpc.StudentServiceImplBase {

    @Override
    public void getStudentInfo(StudentRequest request, StreamObserver<StudentResponse>
responseObserver) {
        // Simulate fetching a student from the database
        StudentResponse response = StudentResponse.newBuilder()
                .setId(request.getId())
                .setName("John Doe")
                .setAge(20)
                .setCourse("Computer Science")
                .build();

        responseObserver.onNext(response);
        responseObserver.onCompleted();
    }
}
```

Step 5: Configuring the gRPC Server

In application.properties, set the port for your gRPC server:

```
grpc.server.port=9090
```

Now, start the server using the StudentServiceImpl class as the gRPC service.

Step 6: Creating a gRPC Client

To consume the gRPC API, you'll create a client with ManagedChannel and StudentServiceGrpc.StudentServiceBlockingStub.

```java
package com.example.student.client;

import com.example.student.grpc.StudentRequest;
import com.example.student.grpc.StudentResponse;
import com.example.student.grpc.StudentServiceGrpc;
import io.grpc.ManagedChannel;
import io.grpc.ManagedChannelBuilder;
import org.springframework.stereotype.Component;

@Component
public class StudentClient {

    private final StudentServiceGrpc.StudentServiceBlockingStub stub;

    public StudentClient() {
        ManagedChannel channel = ManagedChannelBuilder.forAddress("localhost", 9090)
                .usePlaintext()
                .build();
        this.stub = StudentServiceGrpc.newBlockingStub(channel);
    }

    public StudentResponse getStudentInfo(int id) {
        StudentRequest request = StudentRequest.newBuilder()
                .setId(id)
                .build();
        return stub.getStudentInfo(request);
    }

}
```

Now, you can call this client to retrieve student information.

Running the gRPC Server and Client

To test the application, create a REST controller to expose an endpoint that invokes the gRPC client and displays the student information:

```java
@RestController
public class StudentController {

    private final StudentClient studentClient;

    public StudentController(StudentClient studentClient) {
        this.studentClient = studentClient;
    }

    @GetMapping("/student")
    public StudentResponse getStudent(@RequestParam int id) {
        return studentClient.getStudentInfo(id);
    }
}
```

Conclusion

This chapter explored the basics of **gRPC** and how it differs from traditional REST APIs. We walked through setting up a Spring Boot project to use gRPC for efficient communication with our **Student Management API**.